D1175570

AUTUMN DIALOGUES

Autumn Dialogues

Ma Xiaoqiu

Eds. Gerard Donovan and Jeannie Yi

Homa & Sekey Books

Paramus, New Jersey

FIRST EDITION

Copyright © 2021 by Ma Xiaoqiu

Library of Congress Cataloging-in-Publication Data
ISBN: 9781622460984
LC publication record is available at https://catalog.loc.gov/

Published by Homa & Sekey Books
3rd Floor, North Tower
Mack-Cali Center III
140 E. Ridgewood Ave.
Paramus, NJ 07652

Tel: 201-261-8810, 800-870-HOMA
Fax: 201-261-8890
Email: info@homabooks.com
Website: www.homabooks.com

Printed in U.S.A.
1 3 5 7 9 10 8 6 4 2

TABLE OF CONTENTS

INTRODUCTION

What follows are the reflections of a Chinese Original, Madam Ma Xiaoqiu.

This book is not a biography, and the chapters are not a complete exploration of any idea—nor do they try to be. Instead, they come together as contemplations on a wide variety of topics. The entries do not follow a logical order, and old themes return just as new themes arrive. In terms of genre, it comes closest to a series of meditations: they are fleeting but specific; they can be read separately or in sequence; they are sparse but paint an indelible picture; they are sometimes poetic, sometimes prosaic; and any conclusions reached are sometimes practical, sometimes aesthetic.

Yet this remarkable person's writing captures the essence of ideas—within objects and memories and stories—in a few brushstrokes.

You will read her thoughts on traditional Chinese medicine, the inherent resilience of the bamboo; the Inner Self portrayed in a mirror; solitude as joy; culture woven into handmade garments, the Phoenix; how vital culture is for both urban and rural communities in China; and a passage of memorable sensitivity describing three women who made an impression on her.

The passages are fleeting, thin, and transient, and yet they remain in the mind long after reading.

Other explorations, more public in nature, discuss the right way to treat employees; internal promotion versus hiring outside talent; the absolute necessity for positivity and focus; and using the 5,000 year old *Tao Te Ching* (also known as *The Book of Changes*) as the practical foundation for the operations of a thriving multinational enterprise.

A deep reverence for Nature and the Cosmos permeates the writing, and her devotion to reading as a way of improving one's prospects in life—as well as her love of film—forms an intrinsic part of this collection. But in the end, we are left with the dominant impression of a wide-ranging concern for the welfare of others—which is consistent with the principles of the *Tao Te Ching*.

Ma Xiaoqiu is a self-made billionaire and the founder and president of the China DYF Group, whose business model is rooted in China's intellectual history.

Not only is she an Original, she comes unfiltered.

For two decades, there has been a powerful literary-academic amalgam at work in the United States, which has become a *de facto* representative of "Chineseness." (I have also seen "Chineseness.") It began with the hugely successful *The Joy Luck Club* and proceeded in multiple iterations from there. As told by Western-born children of Chinese immigrants, these books combined whimsy with familial historical memory—sometimes traumatic—while forging benevolent stories of identity and belonging.

Inevitably, these narratives create a filter through which Western readers experience a China that is deemed authentic, within that genre.

But a culture viewed through the lens of another is not the same culture. Too often, the writing is colored by the lens of an American sensibility. The lens tells the story. The lens creates the focus and frames the narrative. In other words, Chinese culture becomes familiar without getting too close.

For instance, it's possible for the nation of China to exert its own identity in a manner perceived as being *too Chinese* for writers with an American background. That is where foreign-raised writers and Chinese-raised writers may diverge in their points of view. It is not a decision: it is inevitable.

In Madam Ma Xiaoqiu, we don't get "Chineseness"—we get China.

The West and the East view history in vastly different terms.

In the West, history is viewed as a straight line running from pre-history to the present. The progression of time is marked by wars, famous political and military figures, the creation and dissolution of countries, discoveries in medicine, movements in art, philosophy, the ravages of plagues and other natural disasters.

In the East, history is also a line, but that line is a circle.

There are also recorded inventions and wars, art and philosophy. In China, the circle takes the form of a succession of dynasties (e.g., the *Tang, Song, Yuan, Min, Ching*), each of which lasted about 300 years. Each new Empire rose from a turmoil of natural disasters, famine, and war. It signaled a period of sustained prosperity ahead.

More generally in the East, a spiritual "returning" constitutes an important worldview: in this case, what has happened before will happen again. Because we are tied to the material world by the senses, we keep reverting to familiar circumstances. In time, we acquire a greater spiritual awareness and the means to free ourselves from the cycle of birth and death and birth.

The individual and society are interconnected and interdependent on every level.

For thousands of years, the *Tao Te Ching* has formed the underpinning of Chinese intellectual life and law. It still informs examinations required for public office. Although every Chinese person is aware of its existence, many are unfamiliar with it.

To some in the West, the cohesion of philosophy, statecraft, and a way of living represented by this ancient book of wisdom may appear unusual.

It is Madam Ma Xiaoqiu's intention to change that.

Gerard Donovan

THE PATH TO INNER PEACE HAS NO BOUNDARY

Once one opens the book titled *Autumn Dialogues*, one can hardly escape the strong sense of diversification of its topics, as reflected in the titles of its 81 chapters. It seems that nothing is beyond the reach of the author's inquisitive mind, be it spiritual or material, significant or trivial, historical or daily life, each and every one of them has provided a new window to look deeply into oneself, a new piece of the puzzle of life, a new step towards inner peace. The author, Ms. Ma Xiaoqiu, has demonstrated to us, with this inspiring book, as how a conscious mind can be triggered into soul searching process within the realms of culture, religion, philosophy as well as mundane common sense. The book does source its motivation from ancient oriental wisdom, but it requires no more than a simple open mind to appreciate its own beauty and value.

In the chapter titled "Mirror," we are told that the goal of life is to "become like a mirror that rejects nothing and keeps nothing." Yes, would that be so much better if all of us just simply reflect the nature that surrounds us without distortion, not to impose any claims? Would it be the way to maintain tranquility, avoid many self-induced conflicts and anxiety? Granted, be a human it gives us the privilege of acting upon our own wills, but in reality, we are often frustrated when our will is checked by our environment, which then leads to pain and suffering. Ms. Ma points out for us that if we behave like a perfect mirror, we could have saved ourselves a lot of troubles that are caused by a storming mind.

Autumn Dialogues is indeed a unique book, with its wide-range of topics and some rather intriguing narratives. It might appear somewhat disorganized in terms of subjects presentation, or story-telling, as its subjects jump from chapter to chapter periodically. But that actually enhances the message that it is trying to deliver: everything surrounding us can be the conduit for our own spiritual health!

Publisher's Note

1. My Story with Movies

When I was a child in China, going to the movies was far less common than it is today. There were few films available for people to watch, and cinemas were often makeshift structures erected outdoors. Nothing like the lavish productions and movie hall palaces of today.

Despite the primitive viewing conditions, movies still proved to be a huge attraction. Word spread fast whenever a show was about to begin. Entire families had early dinners; they gathered chairs and hurried in small groups to the venue, hoping to get a good vantage point. Even before the film began, the small rituals of family life were set aside for the excitement of this special occasion.

In the West, most people are familiar with the "ice cream man," who drove a van playing music through the streets of city neighborhoods. The sound of the music was like thread drawn by a needle, bringing together the rich and the poor for those few minutes of magic.

When children first heard the faint jingle from a long way off, it was like a clarion call. They ran to their parents and pleaded for the money to buy a cone. By the time the van turned the corner and parked, a crowd had already gathered. Through a sliding screen, you handed over a coin, and a cold ice cream was placed in your hand. On a hot summer day, you had a couple of minutes to eat it before it melted. The entire episode was brief and unforgettably intense.

The old cinema days in China were a long way from ice cream vans in the city suburbs of the West, but the effect on children was precisely the same—because no matter where they live in the world, children possess the same capacity for magic.

With my younger sister in one arm and two stools in the other, I arrived at an open field.

There was a white screen tied at all four corners to trees or telegraph poles. Nearby, a projector and a loudspeaker had been set up.

Chairs were placed on the ground as the crowd filled the open spaces like pixels, forming their own images of delight and anticipation as they waited for the show to begin.

The projector sprang into life and a sent a sharp light over our heads in the evening air. The beam spilled across the screen and formed into shapes of actors and distant landscapes. For me, the legends of heroes, the romance of love stories, and colorful news stories were as if woven into that beam.

The endless delight of a magic quilt unfolding before my eyes.

The shadows on the screen danced with the light across the faces of the crowd. We too were a screen, and on our minds, the future was forming its shapes as each of us thought about how the stories of our own lives would be written.

What would we become, and where would we go?

Magic has been part of film from the very beginning.

In 1838, the first ever photograph of a human was taken by Louie Daguerre of a boulevard in Paris. The photograph required ten minutes of exposure time: even though the street was busy, only one person appears on the photo—a man standing still while getting his shoes polished. Because everyone else was moving about, they literally disappeared.

In 1888, the French inventor Louis le Prince filmed a short black-and-white movie of his wife's family dancing in a garden. These moving photographs appeared at twelve frames per second, too fast for the human eye to separate.

It is the world's first movie.

Soon the film of an oncoming train caused people to jump aside in terror when shown in small theaters on Paris Boulevards.

The magic of moving pictures was more powerful than whatever circumstances I might find myself in, and I was transported to a world of childhood heroes, a special place of the imagination where poverty or wealth were no longer a determining factor in happiness.

On the silver screen, heroes did what heroes were supposed to do. And in the end, even after many setbacks, justice prevailed.

In *Heroic Sons and Daughters, The Eternal Wave* and *The Sparkling Red Star*, I watched courageous people selflessly pursue justice.

The actor Ken Takakura, in *The Call of the Remote Mountains,* became an ideal prince charming for many girls in their first stirrings of romantic love: he was introspective, he had experienced the ups and downs of life, and his natural charisma commanded love and respect.

What deeply impressed me as a child was a scene in which a soldier, Wang Cheng, stands calm as a tree and shouts, "Fire at me!" before going bravely to his death in a hail of gunfire. He sacrifices his life for a cause—and with passion burning in his eyes.

That passage has given me the courage to overcome many difficulties in my life since then.

History, culture, emotion, and experience—all live within the wonderful world of images. The charm and power of film awakens the perception, it enlivens our sense of beauty and establishes an enduring atmosphere that intoxicates viewers long after the show has ended. Movies can change the world for the better. They can shape the personalities and hearts of countless millions. And yes, they can cultivate in the hearts of the young a sense of personal dignity.

I used to love movies so much. They had everything I longed for: heroism, integrity, kindness, simplicity, purity, selflessness, and beauty. The screen brought those images and stories and characters into my life. I laughed and cried with every adventure. I dreamed a romantic dream that lay dormant in my heart.

After decades of economic reforms, material life has improved dramatically in China. Yet the movies have strayed from the storytelling art. Instead, they showcase greed, eroticism, violence, and horror for their own sake.

No amount of head-spinning special effects can camouflage an emptiness of substance.

What was once an unbreakable bond in my life—the love of film—became strained. A luxurious cinema cannot deliver the simple power of faraway adventures played on those screens and projectors in the open fields.

Technology is not storytelling. Storytelling is not technology.

As a general rule, movies embody the spirit and culture of a country. And so, in recent decades, Chinese film has indeed passively reflected the lost hearts of people entirely transfixed by opulence at the expense of spirit. However, the situation seems to be improving. Productions such as *Youth, Forever Young, Dying to Survive* and *Wolf Warriors* have re-ignited in me those childhood feelings. These are films lit with a love of country and the spirit of kindness, which we should not let slip away no matter how far we progress in economic terms. Once gone, these qualities are difficult to regain. As humans living in a fragile world, we can all too easily lose our connection with what's important in life.

Chinese filmmakers are now more attentive to traditional culture, which is an inexhaustible source of material, and this gives me hope for the Chinese film industry. What's national is international: the artistic expression in Chinese film has the potential to reflect the natural wisdom and beauty in Chinese culture.

The fact is that filmmaking has become an integral part of my company. The question remains—how do we create movies that promote the culture of our ancestors and the Chinese experience? How do we depict the concept that President Xi Jinping has put forward: "One world community with a shared future for mankind"? How do we portray the happiness and sorrow of the Chinese people today in films that will influence the next generation and endear them to their Chinese roots?

I look forward to walking with more like-minded partners on the same path.

As China becomes stronger and richer, filmmakers have woken to the possibilities in the Chinese movie market. Not only will this new awareness change the global landscape of the film industry, it will increase the influence of Chinese culture on a global stage. What kind of storytelling legends are we able to create in film? These new challenges have just begun.

The magic in a great story cannot be measured. Its power to change lives is best viewed over a lifetime; in my case, from the first experiences as in the child, to the lasting proof in the woman.

What I received was so much more lasting than the temporary pleasure of ice cream. From movies I experienced the taste of inspiration and hope, I learned the importance of dreams, and saw how justice and virtue come to those who strive for them. I have never forgotten the images of my childhood and the simple places where I first encountered the glory of cinema.

2. On Reading

People are so busy these days.

Whenever reading comes up in conversation lately, I hear how useless books are; after all, we've done so much reading, yet we haven't managed to live such excellent lives—so what does reading really have to offer? No one would invest in a company that provided no returns. Why invest time in a book?

Is reading useless?

Over time everyone acquires an educated disposition and the wisdom that comes from decades of experience in business and personal matters. But the act of reading has occupied a position in my life whose true worth cannot be measured by any university degree. I cannot imagine what my life would be like without reading.

Perhaps we should ask the question instead:

What is reading?

Imagine, for a moment, that you desire to study the lives of women in 19th-century England. You could of course read history or consult an economics paper on the role played by women at that era, or perhaps watch a documentary on social life and traditions. You might even consult a dictionary for information on popular fashions.

Or better yet, you could read a novel by Jane Austen.

In an instant, you are transported across time to the speech, the thinking and mannerisms, and the social expectations of a young woman before marriage in 1813.

There are no facts to learn, and yet one absorbs a great deal about the relationships between men and women at the time; how they lived, and how they loved and hoped. The mind naturally absorbs and reflects upon these realities.

Reading is time travel. It is *being there.* The time it takes to turn a page and begin reading is the time it will take you to travel back two centuries. It evokes the cultural essence of a country at the time of its composition and transmits a record of daily life, no matter how long ago.

People get excited these days if they get the chance to tour an elegant old house or watch a new movie. Yet in most homes, elegant or ordinary, there are these miniature capsules that can serve as vehicles of understanding.

You share the mind of this person long dead, who is at that moment alive as you read the words that person composed—the same words!

Reading is free experience. How many lessons do we learn from the classics about human behavior and the everyday issues common to people of all eras?

Think of them as instantly available.

They require no fuel, except imagination. They do not become useless if unused. They can quickly come into service with a little dusting.

Yes, everyone is busy. But the habit of reading must be cultivated and encouraged. Books are never too busy for us. We are too busy for books—but by not reading, we lose more time than we gain.

In my teenage years, as a quiet girl, I enjoyed being alone in a companionship of books. Though I sat in a small room, they allowed me to travel beyond the walls and without a time frame—I crossed histories and oceans in search of life's inviolable truths. I cultivated a moral sentiment based on what I read, and I became a better person because of it. As the saying goes, *Read ten thousand books—travel ten thousand miles.*

The 17ᵗʰ-century poet John Donne could have been referring to a book when he wrote:

It makes one little room an everywhere.

I was fortunate to discover the classics. Their beauty is matched only by their practicality. They have changed the course of my life.

Choosing a right book is just like discovering a wise mentor. See how the characters—the wicked, the kind, the educated, the innocent—speak their lines deal with difficult situations. You can see what would have happened *to you* in that situation. What would *you* have done? This is a free education in human affairs—or depending on the book—on business affairs. You can learn these lessons without enduring the hardships normally required to gain those insights. What a tremendous gift to us! If someone told you they could provide guidance on almost any topic under the sun, wouldn't you be interested?

So why don't people read? How can books be *useless?*

Reading can smooth out deficiencies in our nature. Our innate talents are like natural flowers and trees. Reading teaches us how to arrange them so that they may flourish. I have interviewed a lot of successful entrepreneurs from humble backgrounds. They did not appear to have had a great deal of formal education, and yet they had never stopped learning. They had some experiences at work, and they put other experiences to the test in reading—and they gained twofold in wisdom.

Reading creates an instant perspective. Talented people who do not read a lot may be skillful in specific areas of productivity, but those who study and think diligently always maintain an awareness of wider issues. Reading broadens our visions, enhances our knowledge, and enriches *the way* we think and *how* we perceive the world. People who do not read so much sometimes become too narrow in their focus: that kind of attention is not always a good thing.

At some point, of course, we need to be aware of what we read and its impact on our mental process. Loving books is great, but knowing how to judge a book's quality is like keeping to a healthy diet. Absorbing poorly written books without judgement can lead to puffiness in thought and mediocre conceptions of what constitutes progress in our daily lives.

The methods available for reading have expanded enormously since the turn of the century. For instance, one can read an entire book on a cell phone. The issue with cell phones is the distraction of that small screen that affects how we absorb information—those superficial ideas and flashing reminders, not leaving much room for introspection or systematic thought.

Many young people do read exclusively and rapidly on electronic devices. This I do not advocate. There is no sense of occasion, of intellectual immersion, of a specific and special transmission of ideas. We miss the mindful experience of turning the page and being aware of the book's binding, its fragrance, the texture of the pages.

In addition, books are characters in themselves: they have their own emotional associations that mark passages in our lives. We can remember specific rainy days spent in reading, and even recall the passages we read.

Reading is a process of thinking, of being in place, of attentiveness. Digital words on a small screen generally do not provide that kind of experience. Cell phones have no personalities. They offer data—not words.

Yoga is more than simple physical exercise.

Reading is more than absorbing data.

Ancient monks devised entire systems for memorizing passages for future reference—to them, reading was a method of transport into the world of the spirit and the intellect, and they marked the pages with signs and systems for retaining key points in the memory. In this way, knowledge enters the mind and heart of the reader through repeated exposure.

As the sages once said, "When we are young, we read books as if appreciating the moon through a narrow tube. When we reach middle-age, we read as if we are admiring the moon from a courtyard. In our senior years, we read to see the moon in all its detail, as on a spinning dais."

The more experience we have, the more we can accommodate and understand the experience of others as being closer to our own.

The same goes for the isolated rural districts that have not benefited until recently from the resources available to big-city dwellers. In such remote land areas, entire communities of potential readers may exist in isolation. The cultural needs of these rural places are often overlooked. But it has long been recognized that, 1) culture is an engine for innovation and endeavor, and 2) that cultural coherence already exists in these communities, and reading can quickly result in tangible economic activities, such as festivals or study programs.

Reading creates a powerful means of self-expression—because good readers frequently make good writers.

Self-expression lies at the heart of the New Chinese Narrative.

Books bring us together, as people, and as a culture. They are the fabric from which civilizations are woven.

They deserve our respect and attention.

3. The Significance of the Small

Time passes, and the story of *Autumn Dialogues* continues. Starting in January 28, 2019, the book has sailed into the hands of readers like so many birds landing in parts far and near. I have received many letters, even long articles, and been moved by the profound and affectionate sentiments they revealed.

More and more people are beginning to return to *Tao*, which represents an ancient wisdom of social and personal ethics in the context of a constantly changing universe. While walking this path, I have been writing one step ahead of my readers.

To create an opportunity for like-minded people to connect with each another, I hosted a meet-and-greet for readers in Shenzhen, on May 11, 2019, under the theme: "The Significance of the Small."

For me, this meeting with readers was a chance for powerful brainstorming. It was brilliant, it was emotionally exhilarating. Yes, I am an emotional and passionate person, and that side of me comes to the fore whenever I communicate with people who share the same ideas and values as I do.

We are all running at speed towards our dreams, and since I was speaking with people of my own country, I shared with them how impressed I was when President Xi talked about how the Chinese people were "dream-catchers." With eloquence like that, he has given wings to a Chinese aspiration and has pointed out a direction for the future. We belong to a national family of writers, artists, scientists. It's appropriate to be proud of that.

I grew up reading the acclaimed stories of the selfless doctor-without-borders, Norman Bethune, who traveled to China to cure wounded soldiers during the war with the Japanese, and a common solider, Zhang Side, who gave his life to save his fellow soldiers. I was affected deeply by the film *Heroic Sons and Daughters* and the film's signature line, "Fire at me!" These heroes sowed the seeds of a national pride in my heart at a young age. Now, in such better times, I want to devote my energies to promoting Chinese culture worldwide.

Going into that meeting, I hoped that my sincerity had come across to my readers: the overwhelming response suggests that it did.

In the Q&A following the discussion, I discussed the twists and turns of life in terms of the open-focus concept of action through "inaction," and explained what national confidence entailed by referring to a staggering cultural legacy of five thousand years.

These chapters are the result of my own past years of "dream-chasing"—from 1988, when I was in Haikou, a Chinese coastal city, all the way to the City of New York in 2018. Thirty years have been condensed into *Autumn Dialogues*: it is the product of hard-won experience, effort, and hindsight.

The themes are many, and the style ranges from informal to formal. There will be some repetition. That is the nature of a series of meditations. I strive for an overall effect, and I hope that these pages will touch you and bring you joy and inspiration.

Reading good books is like finding helpful friends. Rereading books is like reuniting with long-lost friends. I look forward to discovering more old friends along the way—for *Tao*, and the dreams we hope to catch as an ancient culture.

4. Smell

Due to an acute sense of smell, I was called "army dog" by my father when I was a child. Being so sensitive to any one sense is a double-edged sword; for example, I am now over-sensitive to any artificial scent. A perfume that smells pleasant to others will make me cough and my eyes tear up. However, that same olfactory acuteness also helps me capture natural fragrances that others may not detect.

A species of flower unknown to me grows in the community complex where I live. It looks frail, with pure white flowers like small grains of rice—stars among surrounding bright flowers. They give off a fresh fragrance. It is faintly discernible, yet it becomes even fresher from a distance, gaining in vitality. Later, someone told me that this is the species *Aglaia odorata*.

This poem by Yuan Mei seems to be a good description:

"Where the sun does not shine, a touch of spring naturally comes. The flowers are as small grains of rice, yet they flourish like peonies."

Such a tiny and inconspicuous flower; yet so resilient. The grains are filled with a life-force.

As a child, I was fond of all kinds of plants—I planted my own tree. But I was particularly passionate about flowers, and I longed for my own garden. With the schedule I have now, I don't have the time to take care of a garden—even if I had one. All I can do is to enjoy the flowers I see.

I have no regrets, because deep inside, I already have a garden. With the energy of the fragrance of a flower, I try to live as if in a paradise of freshness and light that reaches all the way to the sky. It enables me to sense the *Tao*.

To access the subtle world of the senses, one adopts habits of *cleanliness* and *silence* inside. Even the slightest look or expression of another can act a channel toward understanding, which encourages good judgement and better results in everything we do. That is reflected in *The Tao following the nature*.

To keep my spirits light, I recite the *Tao Te Ching* whenever I take a walk; and when I sit quietly, I recite the *Heart Sutra* or the *Sutra of Tranquility*. I never do this with over-deliberation—it is just a natural reaction on my part to being still for a moment. Once I enter this state of mind, a sense of awareness emerges all on its own.

There are many manuscripts in my room that record my inspirations and meditations. Through countless reflections and the editing process, a complete work has evolved, which includes the *Autumn Dialogues* series.

Flowers and fragrance store very concentrated levels of energy, which is a path to awakening.

It is the path of the ancient sages.

Tao lies in everything.

5. Mirror

People complain of troubles and the irritation they endure in their daily lives.

They desire to escape their current situation.

In a time of relative tranquility, when no great difficulties burden people, everyone wants to debate at leisure some great truth or other. But when a troublesome event occurs, it causes aggravation, worry, ignorance, and even greed. All their troubles are attributed to some external cause. Everyone blames everything and everybody but themselves.

In fact, people feel annoyed due to their own selfishness. It's difficult for us even to perceive such selfishness, let alone deal correctly with the emotions involved. It is way more convenient to believe that problems can be solved by changing our environment. But if we change our environment, we only acquire temporary relief—the essential problem remains unsolved.

We are still there.

Because the mind remains the same, the old manner of how it views the world remains the same. Wherever one goes, even if to a temple, this truth holds. The Ancient Greek philosopher Socrates said, "How can you expect your travels to do you any good, when you bring the same *you* with you?"

If a mirror is covered by dust, we see a distorted vision which we believe to be the real Self. If we do not possess to means to correct our false perceptions, we can never see through the dust to the truth of the universe, and of our lives.

Not if we continue to believe that a dusty mirror presents the real image.

The journey of life entails clearing away our misconceptions, just as we clean a mirror that reflects the imbalance and haze inside our state of mind. Correcting ourselves—broadening our horizons—means refining the mind through experience. When we adopt a mentality that makes way for the universe without restriction, we will naturally become peaceful and kind. We will develop good relations with others and conduct our business in a harmonious fashion.

In such a state, life feels joyful. It feels complete.

A true state of freedom does not depend on a certain environment. If you possess a quiet heart, you can live freely wherever you are.

So let's feel grateful to those people and situations in our lives that have made our lives complicated. Let's keep an open focus about adversities, a peaceful heart in setbacks, and a gratitude for every experience. We correct our way all along, just as the small movements of a rudder on a boat guides us upstream.

Lacking a certain foundation can cause confusion in those seeking knowledge concerning the heart. For that reason, we read the Chinese classics to learn from the sages, and so emerge into a new understanding of life.

Eventually we become like a mirror that rejects nothing and keeps nothing.

When events occur in our lives, we respond; when they are in the past, we forget about it. We show the same respect to a King and to a Beggar—and gain true freedom.

6. The Heart Sutra

There is a Buddhist classic called the *Heart Sutra*. It contains 260 characters, and it meditates upon two issues: the world we live in—and what it is—and how to view this world and ourselves—because we live in it.

People often talk about the *Heart Sutra* in terms of a journey to the West. In fact, Xuanzang, the Monk, did not receive the Sutra *after* his the journey from the "Western Heaven"; the *Heart Sutra* was a spiritual armor that helped him overcome hardships and dangers on the way *to* the West.

Why do I say this? Legend says that when Xuanzang crosses a sandy river on his way to the West, a gale begins to blow, accompanied by ghosts and terrifying screams. Xuanzang is frightened. He sits cross-legged and recites the *Heart Sutra*. As soon as the ghosts hear this enchanted prayer, they disappear.

Could there really have been ghosts?

It could be said that there are demons in our heart. But other factors exist.

On the way to the West, Xuanzang encounters extreme geographical environments that present real challenges to his physiology. In addition, he is travelling alone. The combination of loneliness and fear for a lengthy period are beyond what ordinary people can tolerate. Whenever Xuanzang finds it difficult to keep going, he sits sit cross-legged and recites the *Heart Sutra*.

In this way, the Scripture accompanies him to the West. It leads him to his destination—and success.

All things are created by the heart. The chaotic exterior world is nothing but a representation. Once we calm down, all returns to quietness.

How could the *Heart Sutra* calm the heart and dispel these "ghosts" and enable Xuanzang to complete his long march of thousands of miles? The answer lies in the approach.

It reveals that the world is in a process of constant change.

People are obstinate.

For instance, we pursue stable careers and stable relationships, while at the same time we worry about birth, senility, sickness, and death. People's rigidity contravenes the laws of nature. As the result, suffering is born.

How to deal with this suffering?

From the *Heart Sutra*:

"No eye, ear, nose, tongue, body or mind, no form, sound, smell, taste, touch or object of mind; no realm of the eyes, no realm of consciousness; no ignorance, nor its extinction, no old-age and death, nor their extinction. There is no suffering, no cause of suffering, no extinction, no path, no wisdom and no attainment."

People endure a lot over the course of a lifetime because of the "six roots" (eye, ear, nose, tongue, body and mind). They are the channels through which people receive information from the external world, contained in "the six objects" (form, sound, smell, taste, touch and mind). From these, all kinds of feelings are generated—greed, anger, foolishness, bad intentions, and lust (the five evils), which are the source of these various irritations, which inevitably generate suffering.

In such a state, people stray from the right path. By relinquishing our rigidity, we can rid ourselves of suffering.

Once we have defeated our obsessions and endless desires, and when we accept the fact that the world is undergoing *constant change*, we learn to move with those changes and embrace those changes.

Then the anxiety will disappear.

The last paragraph of the *Heart Sutra* is an incantation.

Generally speaking, incantations in Sanskrit are mostly transcribed. But this incantation contains a very touching, beautiful sentiment:

"*Gate gate, paragate, parasamagate, bodhi svaha*!": "Go, oh let's go together to the other bank, to the bank of boundless joy and wisdom."

7. Reflection

I had a lot of questions when I first read the *Heart Sutra*. I do not depend on annotations when I read the Classics; instead, I try to comprehend through experience. Then I read it again, examine it again, and practice it again. Through the repetition of this process, I finally came to an understanding of each sentence.

For instance, here is the first sentence in the *Heart Sutra*:

"When Avalokitesvara Bodhisattva practices the profound *prajna paramita*, the Bodhisattva perceives that the five skandhas are empty."

I remained confused for a long time as to why it was "*Avalokitesvara* (guan zi zai) Bodhisattva." One day, when I was writing *Autumn Dialogues*, I had an intuition.

All external things are the projection and reflection of what is inside us. Therefore, if we want external things to change, the only way for that to happen is if we change the source of the projection—or the inside: the heart.

If you pay attention only to the external image, you cannot see the essence of things. You experience obsession, confusion, fear and suffering, the so-called "delusions." In this case, no matter how hard you try to see through the fog, you will not find a path. Only when you look within can you find the origin.

Once the source changes, the external environment changes.

What does "guan" (observing) mean? The answer: use the heart. We "look" through the eyes, but when we do it through the heart, that is "observing." Discovering by means of the eyes we refer to as "seeing," as opposed to "observing."

In "guan zi zai Bodhisattva," *guan* means observing and inner reflection. We turn inward the eyes that have been looking to the outside.

If the world at any moment is without any light—there is complete darkness. People and objects can be seen only if we turn on the lights—the act of "perceiving." We will see the true forms of things when we use the heart. The light returns.

Why practice the Classics? To reach for a unity of knowledge and action. The purpose is to correct our incorrect perceptions, to improve the inner Self. When the inner source of projection changes, all images change.

The best path is to seek the cause of all things in ourselves; to perceive our belief system in external images and then to reverse that image. *Quan zi zai* is the process of improving ourselves at every moment and gaining in wisdom.

The path (*Tao*) exists not in the mountains and remote places; it exists here and now, in the smallest forms of our lives.

These feelings are not gained through annotations and intellectualisms, but through practice in the *here and now*. Without practicing, we won't realize meaning, no matter how many annotations and notes we read.

The real unity of knowledge and action is practice, and inner reflection improves with practice. That way brings us closer to truth.

8. Ugly

How ugly are you?

If I had been asked this question when I was a child, I would have felt terrible. But it's an interesting question to share with my colleagues. Today, the answer would be: "Well, I do find myself beautiful—why not?"

During a casual talk, I thought of *Jane Eyre*, my favorite book from my teenage years. A sentence from it reads: "You are a beauty in my eyes, and a beauty just after the desire of my heart—delicate and aerial."

Most girls are sensitive about their appearance. I was unhappy about my looks and harbored a lot of doubts. I was far from being a confident person. I am so grateful to the character of Jane Eyre, who was a beam of light when I began to shape my personality, my inner self and aesthetics. She helped me to understand at the time that though I was "poor, obscure, plain and little, I could still shine because of my soul." Without a soul and an inner beauty, an attractive appearance is nothing but superficial skin.

One of my employees may serve as an example. Ig judged by the standards of magazine covers and popular culture, she may look plain; but I find her to be very beautiful. She is a girl like Jane Eyre. Unfortunately, the brilliance that glows from the inside her is sometimes lost on others.

What really determines the charm of a person is not appearance, but refinement. A beautiful disposition will make a person appear graceful, well-educated, and well-mannered.

Inner beauty nourishes the appearance and a smartness in mind. With harmony inside and grace outside, our inner world is constantly nurtured. Tempered by time, a type of excellence gradually reveals a person's real charm.

Imagine that an elf lives inside everyone: pretty, smart, and with the grace of a lotus. It hides whenever you blunder or act inauthentically; but when you are calm and pure, the elf reappears.

This is the beauty that belongs in everyone. It is as bright as the sun and as pure as the moon. If someone simply mimics the beauty she sees in others, she can only become a strange mixture of many things—none of them really what she hopes to be.

Great beauty is the result of a constant process of self-cultivation. What looks casual in your eyes might be the result of unimaginable efforts at improvement on the part of another person. If you keep enriching your inner Self, after much austerity you will shape the deepest beauty—and that beauty is exclusively yours. You will never experience envy, and you will have no need to copy others.

You will walk confidently and freely in the world.

9. Morning Meeting

NOTE—*This piece was read aloud at the 3,000th morning meeting*

"My dear friends, once again we are gathered here on such a beautiful day! Over the past ten years, we have met each other like this three thousand times. I am grateful to you all for supporting me. As a result, I have continued my own self-improvement, becoming a better person to serve the great ambitions I have for this company.

Three thousand gatherings of hearts have witnessed the time we have spent together and the stories we have written together. During these ten years, we have walked on the thinnest ice, and we have endured the most challenging circumstances. Yet I have long been accustomed to these constant changes.

If there is one thing that remains unchanged in this world—it is change itself. "

Sometimes I have deliberately put myself in a situation where change becomes *necessary*. For example, in our daily morning meeting, sometimes I don't know what I am going to share before I step onto the stage.

No rehearsal, no script.

And that might be the most attractive part of it. Not to fear making a mistake; nor do I try to conceal any knowledge and insights. All things happen naturally and flow truthfully.

This is who I am: Ma Xiaoqiu.

The hardships and adversities, as well as the slanders and attacks on our company, may look like a slap in the face today; but by tomorrow they will be a handful of pixie dust. With Ancient wisdom as our corporate operational daily guidance, what we have experienced is what we should go through, ups and downs, to get where we are today.

Developing the habit of reading the *Tao Te Ching* every day will accumulate great benefits. Do one thing repeatedly every day, and we will gain energy from it. We read this classic every day. It may be composed of characters written on a page, but Laozi's wisdom contained in the text is a living entity. When we learn the wisdom of the sages from ancient times and apply it to our lives *today,* we are transferring energy from that time to our time.

How can reading Classics provide energy?

Think of a mobile phone. When I call you, can you see the wavelengths that carry the radio signal? And before the phone rings, do you hear or see anything? Yet when you answer it, you can hear my voice.

Just as Laozi said in the *Tao Te Ching*, the Tao cannot be held, heard or observed, but it can function in our daily lives. Reading this classic transfers wisdom, which is the great gift of our company growth, even in a digital age. Just like a phone that brings a distant voice to your ears, words of ancient wisdom bring nutrients to our corporation and to the refinement of our corporate DNA.

Just imagine: If we allow ourselves to be convinced that setbacks are disasters, we will surely be defeated; but if we regard setbacks as part of the chorus of life and a necessary procedure for growth, we can join it and sing a beautiful song. Once we put down our obsessions of love, hatred, joy, and sorrow, and the false distinctions we make between what is good and bad, our lives will fill with happiness. On sunny days, my life is indeed filled with joy; on stormy days, it is filled with just as much joy. I am able to open my arms with a peaceful mind and embrace the storms and endure the tests.

I find equal rest in bright moonlight and fierce oceans. Nothing deters me from meeting you every morning. Whatever happens, my mind feels implacable.

I have been asked how I can be so diligent in business affairs and yet remain calm. The answer lies in our intellectual heritage. Plants grow and die, stars populate the sky, and the universe never ceases to change. We should live our lives in just the way the universe works: *to keep moving*. We should live our lives with the strength of the Earth, bearing whatever changes may happen. That's the wisdom of the Chinese: "As heaven maintains vigor through movement, a gentleman should constantly strive for self-perfection."

Every single plant and object contains a spirit; every journey taken tells a story.

I have grown accustomed to observing changes in the world, and I no longer grieve when plants wither.

A courage within enables me to say: "I fear nothing!"

I know what I am doing and why I am doing it. There is nothing to fear.

I try to cultivate the heart of a child inside me. In my spare time, I like to be relaxed and have fun with my colleagues.

I am passionate about beauty. This universe is filled with charm, and I find it sad that many people haven't opened their eyes to it. A lot of what I share concerns beauty—the experience and feelings associated with looking and feeling lovely. Beauty is a cure for feeling bereft and bewildered. Even when I am 90 years of age, I will still stand in embroidered dresses and share thoughts of beauty with you.

However, my greatest hope is that what I share here will bring you strength and courage, hope and dreams, joy and freedom. I believe that each of us can strive for self-perfection and engage the world with a moral imperative. This force propels me.

As for my career, the challenges in the future will not be greater, nor smaller, than they are today. Growth and achievement come with the wisdom and courage won by pioneers. The world of the future will see fundamental changes, but it will also belong to the courageous, as it has in the past, does in the present, and will in the future. Time will leave us behind—unless we are pioneers.

My dear friends, joy at first sight may not be as long and pleasant a journey as the nearly 3,000 days we have shared. We retain the goals and aspirations of our first meeting. Over the next 3,000, 6,000 and 9,000 days, I hope we will proceed towards our shared dream, burning with the intensity of a phoenix that survives all tests and is reborn through sheer determination.

It's always a better choice to fly against the wind.

This is something to say: I am not afraid, even if there are ten thousand people standing in my way. I have enough courage for this. I will keep sharing my hopes and dreams until the last moment of my life.

On this fine day, I wish everyone a Happy Holiday. I wish joy to your families.

The mountain is high, the road is long.

Let us walk them together.

10. Cherishing the Past. Embracing the Future

At the beginning of June 2019, the company was about to relocate. We said goodbye to the Luohu Office Building, where we spent eight years. We were moving to Futian Central Area, the business hub.

Colleagues helped with the moving of the company while still engaged with pressing business matters.

I watched as the furniture, paintings and office supplies were carried away from their customary positions; they were re-organized and packed for the move to the new office building. Seeing a place as familiar as home turn so empty, I wonder if you experienced the same mixed emotions as I did:

Such expectations for the new. Yet an unwillingness to leave the old.

Things and spaces are tangible. But passion, culture, spirit, and dreams are intangible. For eight years, the tangible and the intangible enhanced each other; they shaped our outward appearance and tempered the inner Self. We leave a small space of a mere hundred square meters and depart for a building of several thousand square meters.

We bring the story of the former building with us, written in those tangible things and spaces; that same story will be recorded in the new corridors and offices.

We forget nothing.

Eight years of growth and development. Eight years of toil, tears and laughter.

The storms we have endured, the difficulties we have overcome, the journeys we have shared. When the time comes to say goodbye, departure evokes strong feelings. I lost sleep the night before. This is the same experience of parting I knew in my childhood.

Since those days I have been highly imaginative and nostalgic.

My father worked in a factory established for military preparedness and civil emergencies. Because of the changes sweeping the nation, we were obliged to move from Chengdu to a small city.

The feeling of parting I experienced at that time is exactly the feeling I have at this moment.

I was unwilling to say goodbye to my relatives; to the sky; to the fields, the crops, my friends, the loving old lady living next door, and even the cats, dogs and flowers in the courtyard. How I wished I could leave with a handful of earth, so that the feeling of home could always stay with me.

My father always required that we go to bed at nine o'clock. The emotions of moving from my home made it difficult to fall asleep. In the darkness, I wrote down the feelings that ran through my mind.

Outside the window, night had fallen.

The sky was filled with stars, and their sparkling recorded what lay below in this child's imagination.

The Sichuan Basin was vast. I could see snowy mountains in the distance under the sun; I could see the horizon where the sky touched the earth. I believed that if I walked to the horizon, I could touch the sky.

In my thoughts, I began my journey with a group of my friends.

We kept walking and walking, only to find that the world was much larger than we thought, and that the horizon was much farther than what it seemed, and that the people were much smaller than I had believed.

But in the tender heart of that child, an essential emotional backdrop formed that has remained throughout my life.

I was filled with the courage to explore, and I held a dream inside me large enough to touch the stars.

My family used to live close to a train station. On the platform, people constantly met and parted.

Railways are the recorder of stories.

I have had intense emotions about railways that extend to remote places and to unknown futures. Whenever I used to think of such places, and the journeys undertaken by so many people to places so far away, I would silently weep. This might be a sensibility with which I was born.

These events of decades past are deeply engraved in my mind. Sometimes they appear before me like silent movies. These memories bring the distinct hue of experience into my daily existence. The feelings I retain from my childhood are not so much related to my life as it was at home. They have formed emotions and experiences that sustain my life. They are the guiding beam of a lighthouse on a rocky shore, and they enable me to better understand my own life and work, and that of others.

I am convinced that these sensations and sensibilities are connected to the heavens and earth and human beings. I believe that real artists can tune into such feelings that others may not experience to the same degree. They touch the world with their art.

Once again in my life, I have felt the sorrow of parting.

The process was recorded in my camera: many unforgettable stories come with us to the new office building. We shall not forget the past. Beautiful memories are the lifelines of our existence; they transform into actions. Even after reviewing the past, we should be aware that time waits for no man.

We must now start a new journey. We have many great things to accomplish.

The years we spent here have laid a solid foundation for our business and our mission. This moment ends the first chapter in an Epic. It has been a brilliant chapter, and yet it has ended.

We turn the page. We step onto a new stage and embrace a splendid, magnificent future.

11. The Beauty in Creation

The sky silently observes us.

Some people are born with an appreciation for the abundant beauty of creation that the night sky represents. That glorious sight never fades, regardless of how many times we view it.

I used to be a tomboy in search of adventure and exploration; I would climb trees, jump off the roof and fight with others. That, I guess, is part of the creativity in children: an active curiosity about the world that drives them to keep searching and discovering. When older, I became more creative. I changed how the furniture was arranged in the house, making my own curtains, pillows, sweaters and clothes—whatever took my fancy.

My father has kept the pillows I made and takes them out every now and then.

Training the mind and keeping up our creativity is a good habit to have.

I once took lessons in writing poetry, which covered techniques in composing. They taught students to draw objects while reflecting on them. The poems seemed to flow naturally. What I learned was the importance of using my hands to engage my mind. As people depend more on cell phones and computers, their mental faculties are not being exercised.

Technology makes our lives more convenient, but that convenience comes with a price.

The Internet delivers a nonstop flow of distracting information. Our attention is sidetracked by data to the extent that it is difficult for most people to finish reading a book, like a runner tiring halfway through a race. Our minds are being shaped into warehouses of information—but information is not knowledge. As we outsource our faculties, we become passive receptacles for data, most of which has *no relevance to our lives*.

Efficiency has been elevated to a status is never had before, and humans are being demoted to recipients of temporary pleasure. In fact, we are abandoning what makes us human—the joy of thinking deeply and creating actively as higher primates—in the service of convenience. This is exactly the opposite of what we should be doing. Knowledge requires effort and concentration.

Our ancestors, as described in books of the time, had strong physical functions. As technologies become more and more advanced, and we keep relying on digital devices instead of employing our hands as they were meant to be used, they will gradually shrink and lose their intended function. Some scientists believe that in two hundred years, humans will be significantly overweight but have long, thin fingers.

The world-famous futurist and business consultant Alvin Toffler, who was admired in China, correctly predicted in his two best-selling books *Future Shock* (1970) and *The Third Wave (1980)*, that we would be overwhelmed with choices in a new information age, and bombarded by increasingly complex networks of data. He coined the phrase "information overload." (*The Third Wave*, together with a documentary, were best-sellers in China and distributed to schools. In 2006, *The People's Daily* named him one of 50 foreigners who shaped modern China.)

The joyful moments in our lives are often composed in creation. It is a deeply human enterprise, whether preparing food, devising breakthroughs at work, handicrafts, concentrating on studies—these things always bring us the kind of lasting satisfaction that online dramas, games, *Tik Tok* videos and other like entertainments cannot provide.

Be mindful.

Concentrate on what you are doing, tasting, seeing, touch at this moment. How green this leaf. How sour this fruit. The feel of hardwood under the fingertips. Connect yourself with the world around you. Try to stop being consumed by the information you think *you* are consuming. With a tranquil mind, concentrate on what you are doing at this very moment, feel the process of creation.

Enjoy the miracle of doing.

12. Bu Da Ya Yue, the Sound of Bliss

—The headset concert begins. Once again, we gathered here. Everyone is quiet.

With the headset covering our ears and our eyes closed, we hear the piece "Bu Da Ya Yue."

Music is the most sophisticated language in the world, because it contains no words. It speaks directly to the heart. It jumps and flows, narrating an ancient joy and sorrow.

Music has nowhere to return to and nothing to rely on; likewise, we are wanderers in this universe.

Music from the bamboo flute reaches the deepest part of the heart. Notes from the Zhongruan and the Daruan flow. They reach us, flowing in a seamless space.

A lost child feels pain and joy when hearing the call of his mother.

Tears as warm as sunlight in Autumn days.

In the embrace of such warmth, you do not need to be strong. I do not ask you to give me anything.

As the elegant music rises, the tender sadness inside embraces all living creatures like a tender hand and guides them out of their suffering. The power of music is the power of creation—we are present at the beginning of our own lives. We are present at the moment we took our first breath, like the breath that issues from the bamboo.

The road ahead is long. Such sad and deep-reaching music sings about the long journey that we have had together, and I will say my hello and goodbye along all the hills and streams I have passed in this life.

We walk out of selfishness and let go of our narrow views. When love is all about giving, you don't have to worry about losing.

You must be so blessed to meet a person who can wake you up the way this music wakes me.

Bu Da Ya Yue, the sound of bliss.

13. Movement, Stillness

Lotus flowers grow in sludge, yet they are astonishingly clean and beautiful.

During the Civil War, the resistance kept close to their enemies but kept their political goals clearly in their minds. They knew what to do and what not to do. They understood the line that separated them from the people they fought against.

They achieved a balance of movement and stillness, of action and inaction.

It is hard to follow the disciple of the lotus flower that "mixes with light and remains in harmony with the dirt."

Modern physics understands the relativity in movement. All things move reference to other objects. Taoism conforms perfectly to the laws of the universe, which tells us that stillness is nothing but a state relative to movement.

We know that what we see as a desk is actually mostly empty space held together by kinetic energy: spinning atoms and the elements spinning within them. The daylight we see is mostly dark—the photons of light move so quickly, at over 300,000 kilometers per second, that we see these tiny photons as being one solid sheet of light.

In reality, there is darkness between the photons.

In the solar system, moons circle planets, planets circle the sun, and the sun, like a carousel with its planets, journeys around the Milky Way galaxy. The galaxy meanwhile is being approached by its nearest neighbor, Andromeda, over four light years away.

In billions of years, our two galaxies will mix.

As Alvin Toffler said, "Change is not merely necessary to life—it is life."

Our thoughts are ceaseless and loud, like monkeys in the trees.

We are distracted by the movement of the "six dusts": form, sound, smell, taste, touch and imagination, which appear through the "six roots": the eyes, ears, nose, tongue, body and mind. Our senses are like a magician who creates illusions we think represent what has happened. Delusions are generated because we don't know what links those movements.

Tao—emptiness, nothingness, stillness.

The *Sutra of Quietness* says that with "a still mind, the whole world settles." Taoism doesn't seek to restrain desires nor ignore them. An optimal point of balance leads to a state of harmony.

The spinning atoms are invisible, but they hold together the desk at which we sit, reading a book.

14. Wisdom of an Ancient Love

The girlfriend of a celebrity checks his cell phone, and their 9-year relationship ends. A hubbub of criticism and discussion flares up in the media and social platforms.

During a meet-and-greet for *Autumn Dialogues,* I was asked whether people should check each other's cellphones.

I have experienced marriage and several relationships. My opinion here is that we should check the phone of our partner if we want to. If I have decided to be with you, that's a commitment. I have decided to love you and only you in the rest of my life. If you allow me to check your phone, it shows that there is nothing being hidden from me; but if not, I will not force the issue.

Everyone wants a beautiful love and a happy marriage, but beautiful things are not easily acquired. You should be moderate in your eating habits if you want a slim figure; and being successful in life requires constant effort. The same truth applies to love and marriage. You love the other person heart and soul. If you want a happy marriage, you must put the other person first.

Above all: honesty is everything.

Extramarital affairs seem part of modern love and are never far from the headlines. Young people are giving marriage a second thought, perhaps because contemporary society has placed so much pressure on them, and they have lost a belief-system that a more traditional culture would sustain.

People need structure. We may not like to admit it.

We may consider ourselves independent of any such notions of family or work relationships. But look around you: almost every single person you know forms a part of a structure to which you belong.

Without human structures, humans lose their capacity to function. We are social animals.

The Book of Changes is instilled with thousands of years of experience and knowledge on the part of our Chinese ancestors. It explains the system of the universe; it talks about love.

In the prologue, the book recounts, "First there was the Heaven, from which all things were generated, and from which men and women emerged; then couples; then parents and children."

A sentence in *The Book of Changes* reads "If two people think alike, there is nothing they cannot achieve."

From *The Book of Songs* to the literature of the Tang Dynasty unearthed in Dunhuang, we witness the historical pursuit of love and marriage on the part of our ancestors.

They believed that marriage was the result of great bliss accumulated over many lives, and couples tried their best to make each other happy. They felt obliged to have children and to spend their lives together—even be buried together after death.

Does that sound strange to you—or romantic?

If a couple that has lived together for many years cannot live harmoniously, and their problems have extended into their respective families and even to the neighbors, they're better off facing the fact that they are dry sand being rubbed between two hands. Cohesion is never going to happen.

The best choice is to go their separate ways—decently—and sincerely wish the best for one another.

Cell phones are minefields in matters of love.

The frequent explosions we hear all over the media are proof of a self-centeredness that wants the best of both worlds: the happiness of marriage and the pleasures of an extramarital affair.

It harms the other person, the cheaters themselves, the children, the parents, and in many respects, society as a whole.

It's not easy for a man and a woman to meet in this life, and it's even more difficult to become a couple. In the evolution from strangers to friends and partners in life, trust grows from honesty. For some people, a traditional outlook is the right answer because of the structure and networks of support it provides.

A happy life is of benefit to everyone.

15. The Most Beautiful Women

All women want to be beautiful.

In my view, the word *beauty* itself is the synonym for women, and every woman is beautiful. Why, in the eyes of beholders, do some people appear beautiful and others less so? That depends on a sense of awareness and cultivation.

A woman can possess beauty, elegance, and character if she is sensitive, fearless and calm. The most beautiful women are often the most confident ones. Their self-confidence grows from an inner strength rather than their appearance or other external conditions. It originates in a vast world that people can't see.

When I was a child, I regarded Sister Aqing, from Shajiabang, as an idol. She looked like an unassuming common country woman, but she was fearless, and she confounded her enemies with a calm and witty mind—which enabled her to solve one crisis after another. Handling things deftly was born of self-assurance, and I saw in her an astonishing beauty.

A female singer with a beautiful voice once sang a song for a mentor, who was deeply touched by her voice, and said: "If you learn to ignore your protruding teeth when you sing, you can conquer the whole world with your songs." While it was direct, it had the desired effect. The singer learned to ignore her condition and concentrate completely on singing. In the end, she attracted a worldwide audience with her talent and unique charm.

Beauty is a reflection of personality. Only when you feel comfortable with yourself can your charm manifest itself, which has absolutely nothing to do with your appearance.

Beauty is not the privilege of young people.

There are those who become more charming as they get older. Qin Yi, a famous film actress, looks extraordinarily attractive with gray hair; Fu Ying, a female diplomat, has the sweetest smile in the world, and any wrinkles are part of that sweetness and beauty. One particular sense in a person can accentuate her beauty.

A voice. The way she moves her hands.

More diverse standards of beauty are emerging. We can each bravely show our unique beauty, and the light in us, to the world.

Some people assume they have no relationship with beauty because they are not "good-looking," or because they are no longer young. They abandon themselves before the world does so, and they go on to muddle through their lives. Some girls believe that "an ugly girl is worse than a dead one" and spend all their energy trying to make themselves look more attractive. They hang out with friends in the hope of finding an ideal man to marry. All these misunderstandings are a waste of their lives.

I am not trying to suggest that outer beauty is unimportant.

All I want you to think about here is that beauty is not only about appearance but also found in attitudes and manners; it is a natural reflection of cultivation and mature thought. A person's demeanor is the combination of appearance, thoughts, spirit, education, and cultivation. Outer beauty truly touches people when accompanied by inner charm.

Remain aware. Maintain a lifelong motivation for learning, especially reading, and being true to who you are. Then

you are already beautiful, and you will stay beautiful throughout your life.

16. My Sun. Your Sun

At the UN General Assembly Headquarters, I gave a speech titled "Chasing the Sun in My Heart." The title refers to my inheritance as a child, the depth and richness of my own Chinese culture, in much poorer circumstances and so far away from the grandeur of that stage.

That is "the sun in my heart."

Those in the audience were also far removed from the open fields of my childhood: there were celebrities, statesmen from around the world, and journalists from the major news media such as CBS, NBC, and FOX.

The UN is a microphone to the world.

I was somewhat anxious before the speech. I wasn't sure how much material would emerge intact from the simultaneous interpretation, which requires and instant decisions from the interpreters due to the pressure of time.

I have heard that to translate one language into another, you must sometimes translate not the actual words, but the metaphors. That means employing entirely different words to get the same effect in the second language. The idea is interesting: you must go through what is strange in order to reach what is familiar.

My voice at the microphone echoed the tiny voice still ringing loudly from out of my childhood years.

After I finished my story of the *Tao Te Ching*—the book that had accompanied me for ten years—the response of the audience suggested that they had indeed understood the core idea: virtue (*Tao Te*).

Later, I spoke with a journalist who had served as an anchor at Fox News for thirty years.

He said that while listening to my speech, he saw an image from the 9/11 attacks in his mind. He was on the scene that day, as journalists often are—along with firefighters, medical personnel, and the police. He remembered people rushing out of the building as he rushed in. He saw at close range what that disaster really looked like, and remembered years later watching the shining structure where the towers once stood: The Freedom World Trade Center.

When we remember, we are the audience for our own recollections.

A Memorial & Museum represents the resting place for over 2,600 souls whose lives were cut short on that day.

A reflecting pool occupies the space in which they worked. Clean water cascades down the walls. Here, you feel the power of water that also calms the spirit. The city traffic seems far removed, almost in another world. Beside it, the new tower rises. Glass windows merge with the blue of the sky.

We talked awhile, and the news anchor showed the interpreter a phrase from my speech: "The highest good is like water. A man of virtue should be like water flowing and nurturing all other things."

The pool occupies two spheres of time at once. The horror of the past and the calm of the present.

Two-thirds of our planet is water. It's what people see when they view Earth from the moon. They see the light of the sun shining on all that water. From farther out in the solar system, we are "the blue dot." That sun belongs to each country: the light has no boundaries.

Our sun, your sun.

I hope that my talk at the UN created a cultural bridge between our countries with the structure of the *Tao Te Ching*. This treasure of Chinese culture knows no limits in time or space.

There are more than 6,000 high-rise buildings in Manhattan, and 274 of them are over 150 meters tall. Large rock formations under Manhattan provide the load-bearing capacity for this remarkable vista. It represents American power in manufacturing and construction, and a culture of overcoming adversity.

Of the many beautiful edifices in Manhattan, the GM Building is a storied structure with inspiring views.

Two Chinese companies have offices inside: one is DJ.com, the other, DYF Entertainment. Our new dream of China and America working together will grow from here.

17. To Strangers

Mountains are born violently, whether through tectonic collision or volcanos, and yet they create so much of the beauty in our lives. They are awe-inspiring, fragile, and spiritual in their dimensions. A large percentage of the Earth's fresh water originates there. They harbor a rare biodiversity of plants and animals, a rich archeological record, and precious isolation for hermits. Mountain villagers experience fresh, unpolluted air and space to roam.

The haunting Changbai Mountains, in Northeastern China, was the subject of a traditional cultural exchange event in August of 2018 called, "Worshiping the Heaven and the Mountain."

We were fortunate to have as our guest Mr. Zhang Fuyou, the "living fossil" of the Mountains. He is in his 70s and sprightly in his demeanor. He speaks in a powerful voice about the culture of the Mountains. Having studied the region for twenty years, he displays great knowledge and possesses an astonishing memory, which is reflected in the many books he has authored on the subject.

Zhang Fuyou has been acknowledged, with justification, as the cultural pride of Changbai.

He has climbed the mountains over two hundred times on archeology investigations. He is the person who discovered the stone bell and hand-axes that pushed estimated human activity in the mountains back by fifty thousand years.

It would be difficult to overstate this achievement.

In 1948, a Harvard archeologist called Hallam Movius drew an arbitrary line across the world map. This line proposed to divide ancient users of hand-axes (in Europe, Africa, and Western Asia) from tool users in East Asia. The absence of the hand-axe in East Asia was a determining factor. In doing so, he drew inevitable conclusions about a lack of technological skill on the part of East Asians. In discovering hand-axes, Zhang Fuyou destroyed the scientific basis for the "Movius Line."

He mediated a diplomatic incident concerning historical territorial claims between China and Korea, and has shared his knowledge with the well-known cultural and literary figure, Yu Qiuyu.

He was the first to confirm that Li Ji, the Lord of Yang'an on a bronze sword from the Zhao Kingdom, unearthed in Ji'an, Jilin, was Prime Minister during the reign of Emperor Huiwen, and the son of Li Dui, the 36th-generation ancestor of Emperor Taizong of the Tang Dynasty, and the fifth-generation descendant of Li Er—namely Lao Tseu.

His hands bear the wounds and scars from unearthing cultural relics buried in the earth. These hands have captured the history and beauty of the region. They have written his poems.

He has quite a few mysterious stories to tell of his mountain investigations. He has been in the right place at the right time to witness celestial phenomena that can be a particularly beautiful sight in a mountain region.

On Baiyun Peak, the main peak of the Mountains, he saw a halo around the sun—rather like a circular rainbow. Ice crystals were suspended in the clouds and refracted the sunlight to create an astonishing halo, referred to by meteorologists as a Sundog. They can be large and overpowering in effect.

As the ceremony "Worshiping the Heaven and the Mountain" came to an end, the circular rainbow appeared again. He was overjoyed at the timing: "Why does it appear now in front of these people?"

He wrote a poem to celebrate the sight.

The development and protection of the Culture of the Changbai Mountains is a precious process, and even if we were witnessing an astronomical event, Heaven may have felt our sincere intention. There are intangible energies in the Mountains, where material energies and cultural energies integrate. That is the energy that has attracted generations to set foot in these mysterious heights.

Zhang Fuyou has said, "We finally have a chance to face our mysterious past, as if entering the realm of dreams, a place of living fossils that need us to discover, interpret, praise and protect them."

Changbaishan History & Culture Park is a project to which the group attaches great importance. We hope to do our bit in rescuing and protecting the intangible cultural heritage of the Changbai Mountains, and make them a cultural locale, and in doing so, pass on a wealth of new historical knowledge about those who lived their lives here, long ago.

"I do feel, my dear stranger, that I have been extended in your existence."

This 14-word poem by Alfonsina Storni is the best expression of our intention to protect the culture of Changbai. A culture can only survive its heritage is handed down to generation after generation of strangers.

Mountains have peaks at which you may arrive and depart, but a road knows no end. In his 70s, Zhang Fuyou ignores illness and pain. He continues his journey in these mountains towards the ancient culture that came before us.

We, too, are on the way.

18. Being Busy

The speed at which time passes often appears relative to how busy we are at any given moment. It accelerates in the background when we are absorbed in work—a form of Zen—or as the mythologist Joseph Campbell called it, "our Bliss." We look up, surprised—we thought it had stopped—but we achieved so much.

If we are impatiently waiting on a platform for a train to arrive, each second takes ten seconds to pass.

A week has passed in the twinkling of an eye.

I always need to be doing things. In other words, even if it is the weekend as I write this, "doing nothing" is not an option.

As a child, I consciously used time to foster the habit of learning.

I taught myself to sing, dance, make clothes, cook, read and write. Thanks to this habit of learning, I find myself doing different kinds of work on any business day.

One of Isaac Newton's Laws of Motion—in plain English—states that the busier you are, the busier you will get. He never said those words. The formula went more along these lines: An object at rest tends to stay at rest. An object in motion tends to stay in motion.

Although his discipline was mathematics, in essence this great scientist was talking about how difficult it can be *to start moving*.

A train requires a certain amount of engine power to roll those wheels from a stationary position into the pounding of a speeding locomotive.

If you experience inertia, finding the necessary motivation to start doing something can be terrifically difficult. It can be a shock, an accident, an unpleasant discovery—sometimes these events can be the very thing that spur us into action.

But once you do start moving, doing the work becomes easier. Things begin to flow. We have many sayings for this phenomenon—because we've all known the difficulties taking that first step to rectify what we've neglected for too long.

Eventually, we have no choice but to begin.

Step Number One. That is how you begin.

My company's offices were located in Pengnian Plaza for a long time. The Plaza's founder Mr. Yu Pengnian reached a ripe old age of ninety, and he was working the day before his death. He did not permit himself a life of pleasure. Instead, he did charity work by helping cataract patients. Probably because of that, Mr. Yu had very good eyesight. When signing the contract with me, he didn't need glasses.

It seems that all masters in the world who lived a long time spent their lives working. Mr. Fang Cheng, a famous master of cartoons in China, was one. When asked for the secret of longevity, he said two words: "Stay busy." Drawing pictures, riding a bike, taking care of his flowers—always doing something, Mr. Fang.

It is not easy to direct your intention outward, away from the fulfilment of our own wants.

But if we do all things only for our own enjoyment and benefit, I think it's a breeding ground for laziness. When we do find the courage to break the comfort zone, and to face challenges and difficulties, laziness doesn't stand a chance.

The actor Denzel Washington, explaining why only 2% succeed and 98% do not, listed specific rules for success. One was, "If you're looking for an excuse, you'll find one."

Time, when gone, stays gone. It doesn't add itself to the end of the line and wait for you again.

Each tick of the clock takes away a measure of life. It drains it little by little, slowly but consistently, all the way from youth to old age. It may be true that "an inch of time is worth an inch of gold." In my view, it's worth so much more.

Find solutions instead of excuses. They are located in the same place: your mind.

Don't ask *why*, but rather *what* and *how* and *where* and *when*.

Being busy is the cure for many, many problems.

19. One Rule

When asked by Yan Hui, Zi Gong and Sima Niu what "benevolence" was, Confucius gave three answers. Possibly, each of the questioners had a different understanding of the word, and so the answers were tailored to the specific qualities each had in mind.

The answers may have led to three highly desirable outcomes.

No perfect people exist.

When it comes to discipline within the company, I tend to use different methods to guide different employees. A single rule of thumb won't have the desired effect if applied as a one-size-fits-all approach. It may be easier to adopt such procedures; but that's not our philosophy.

Intentions matter, and so does using the right methodology.

I am particularly hard on some people, and lenient with others. Different measures with the same intention.

Kindness and compassion form the basis of making proper use of talent. Tolerating errors can achieve the impossible. People make mistakes—usually on the way to making something important. Give them time to correct those mistakes. Most will.

It can be difficult for people to see their own problems in good times. Only when faced with an inescapable situation do they reflect deeply on the challenges they face. This management philosophy has helped many to develop into key members of the team.

Team leaders must set themselves up as role models, so that other members can see the standard being set; and when challenged by subordinates, management should reflect on the questions asked.

In our company, there are no rules except one: to study the *Tao Te Ching*, which our employees do every morning.

Another criteria I request is attitude. Attitude is a Ladder leading to a higher ground.

When we are young, we view failure as a complete disaster.

When something goes wrong, we regret the choices we made, and we try to distance ourselves from that event. But in fact, mistakes are a ladder to success if we can understand that how we react to them is the difference between people who prosper, and people who remain stuck.

There are those who choose to retreat after failure—to give up—and there are those who try again.

Remember this. Every experience we have had in life has been both inevitable and necessary for us to grow. Our attitude to failure determines our future.

One of America's founding fathers, Thomas Jefferson, put it this way: "Nothing can stop the man with the right mental attitude from achieving his goal; nothing on earth can help the man with the wrong mental attitude."

Failure is God's gift to us. If you are a talented person, your experiences, whether successes or setbacks, will forge the person you are meant to become. Both positive and negative results are valuable. We can succeed if we embrace these tests of character and are not afraid of difficulties in the future.

The road to success encounters blockade after another.

No matter what qualities people bring to the company, as long as they read the *Tao Te Ching* and possess positive attitude, reflect on it every day, and act on it every day, they will become the qualities we value: altruistic, focused and loyal.

Yes, employees have exhibited errors in judgement; but in time they developed great qualities.

20. Rap the *Tao Te Ching*

The *Tao Te Ching* has been an ancient Oriental "wisdom bridge" that has guided the world in the past. It links history with the present and keeps the future in sight. It never grows out of fashion. With five thousand characters, the *Tao Te Ching* explains the laws of the universe, the world, the country, and the heart. The beauty of the wisdom transmitted in the *Tao* has been the source of knowledge to which I and my colleagues have adhered.

In the annual gala of 2018, we greeted the following distinguished guests from overseas: Mr. Porter Bibb, a well-known American business strategist, financier, journalist and writer; Mr. Lorenzo Borghese, prince of Italy, businessman and member of the Borghese Royal Family; Mr. Holmes H. Stoner, founder of the Pacific Rim Chamber of Commerce; and Mr. Philippe G. Damas, Board Director of TMB Bank of Bangkok, ex-J.P. Morgan Asian vice-chairman.

They had come for the *Tao Te Ching*.

In 2018, I visited America twice and brought the book with me. Anywhere I went, I shared with my American friends the fact that our company considered this book as being our management standard, and outlined the results we obtained from it. They were deeply interested—and curious—about the book.

It has always been my dream to be an ambassador for culture, promoting cultural exchanges between China and the

Western world, introducing young people to our heritage, and creating an awareness in foreigners of the wisdom of the Orient.

That being said, "The Tao that can be told of is not the absolute Tao."

In the annual conference each year, I always prepare a performance despite a full schedule. The annual conference in 2018 was attended not only by friends from overseas but also young people. I wondered what kind of performance I should prepare.

I thought: What if we give a modern touch to the *Tao Te Ching* and turn it into a lively and romantic song?

In this way, the rap version of the *Tao Te Ching* was created.

This performance was a medley of *Smiling Above the Clouds*, a rap of the *Tao Te Ching*, and a recital of *Believing Myself*. During the performance, I changed my outfit three times and performed the *Tao* using classical music, rap, and rock.

I first appear on the stage in traditional Zen garments, emerging as if from deepest history, which creates a poetic atmosphere. A song plays. Before the song ends, I change my clothes and become an energetic rapper dancing on stage. This dance routine certainly wins the approval of the audience!

The performance became the most popular in the program. Paul—who owns New York Good News broadcasting and a 30-plus years veteran of CBS Television, suggested it was as good as a Broadway show. He invited me to perform it in America.

Tao was performed in Chunjian Stadium of Shenzhen (akin to the Staple Stadium in LA). The show was shown to the world through live streaming. Within a month, it was viewed over six million times.

I never received any professional training in singing. The closest I came to instruction was a book, *Singing and Practicing,* that I read when I was in primary school. In it, the ABC of Folkstyle singing and *bel canto* was explained. I copied it down and practiced. I am convinced that if we focus on something we really care about—and persist—we can always do well.

The power of *Tao* depends on practice.

The beautiful mysteries in it are tasted through repetition. This performance demonstrated that even through different iterations, *Tao* is always present.

I look forward to attracting more people to feel *Tao,* touch *Tao* and learn *Tao.*

21. Yin and Yang, That's Tao

For the past few days, I have been in Wuhan on a business trip. When I look out from the window every morning, the city is shrouded in haze.

Environmental issues have dominated the agenda from the country's top decision makers to ordinary citizens. In terms of a systematic approach to pollution control, it may take decades of hard work before results become apparent. We are in a process that western countries have been in years before us: excessive development, followed by understanding the problem, followed by decades of effort—and finally remedying the situation.

Improving environmental conditions in Chinese cities is no small task. Rome wasn't built in a day, and the smog will not be cleared in a season. Change accumulates over time.

The *Tao* advises: "Accomplish the great task in a series of small tasks."

If we want the environment to prosper, we need to be conscious of what environmental protection means in our daily lives. That is a process of reflection, not blind numbers on a page.

For some years now, the prosperity that has come to China has lowered a veil over the skyline. When we take a comprehensive view of both human and industrial activities, and act on our findings, that veil will lift—permanently.

We will "know what's happening in the world without stepping outside our doors and see the *Tao* of Heaven without looking out of our windows."

22. The Illusion of Control

A phenomenon exists that is termed *the illusion of control*.

We delude ourselves into thinking we can control the world around us.

In an *Autumn Dialogues* conference, the host asked me my opinion of love.

I said that it is part of human nature to love, and that love binds people in a synchronicity. Everyone longs to be loved, but a need for control soon creeps in as jealousy or possessiveness.

But love can't be possessed. It is an energy.

More specifically, love is a "vibration frequency" between people. While it may appear that we are giving, in fact we are the ones receiving that energy, much more so than we give. You can control an energy as much as you can push back a wave.

There is no cause for reciprocation or analyzing how the other person is treating you. The same attitude applies in the kindness we show all creatures.

Giving selflessly generates energy.

Instead of obsession and control—try emptiness.

When the mind is large enough to hold within it a vast emptiness, like the emptiness that lies at the heart of creation, we link ourselves to a consciousness that is cosmic—our origin. All the deficiencies, the fear and anxiety evaporate. They vanish inside the new perspective.

The Great Void is an unlikely elixir of love.

The energy that flows is more powerful than any force you can imagine.

Allow the mind to dwell in that emptiness. It is our true nature: quiet, vast, inclusive.

If you stop trying to control something that cannot be controlled, you will not experience the frustration of failing. People cannot be controlled. If you think you can do it, you will ultimately fail.

There is no restraining the emptiness that is *Tao*.

23. Understanding Acquired Through the Tao

A passage from *The Book of Changes*: "The Tao never does anything; yet through it all things are done." Think of a circuitry that unifies. On an ordinary everyday level, wires connecting a house and all its parts.

This sentence is essential to understand Chinese culture.

The *Tao Te Ching* teaches that we should "attain the utmost in passivity and hold firm to the basis of quietude." *The Great Learning*, a classic of Confucianism, teaches that "when you know where to stop, you have stability; when you have stability, you can be tranquil; when you are tranquil, you can be at ease; when you are at east, you can deliberate; when you can deliberate, you can attain your aims."

This is a spiritual comprehension all of us were born with. We are unable to acquire complete understanding through a formalized set of instruction. This is not because we understand too little, but because we believe we understand too much.

Understanding and learning are two different words because they means two different things—otherwise we would use the same word. Facts are not knowledge. They block the channels of understanding while claiming to clear them.

It's not "being" but "non-being" that is absent in formal instruction; that lack hinders us from accessing the path to *Tao*.

The following is from *The Book of Changes*: "We can shape clay into a bowl, but it is the emptiness inside that holds what we want."

For that reason, we cannot be at one with the universe even though we have the best teacher guiding us, because the channels and passages are blocked by our own ideas.

Social media is too often a platform for the information overload crowding the electronic domain.

Everyone is an expert.

If I state here that opinions can hinder our progress, people might be incredulous.

Tao says, "When the lowest type of men hear of *Tao*, they break into loud laughter. Otherwise it would not be *Tao*."

Scientists tell us that the behaviors that may have functioned as a child, can damage the adult. You only remember the benefit as a child, and you do not see the damage in the adult.

Tao says something similar. It involves undoing:

"The student of knowledge aims at learning day by day; the student of *Tao* aims at losing day by day."

If you tie a knot on a boat, and the knot slips—you must undo it to save the boat. In this case, undoing is progress. You are moving forward.

Again, the *Tao* is there when it states that a good general knows that an army goes forward by retreating. Yield. Undo the knot, undo the damage that it will cause in the future. Taking the time now prevents a worse situation.

And that is another feature of *Tao*—it is a unified system. What makes sense in one part, makes sense in another—even though *Tao* makes no effort.

Tao emphasis subtraction (removing obsessions) until the state of doing nothing is reached. That is the most potentially active of states, it is an enlivened inaction through which the spirit of the universe flows freely. We will understand what "understanding through induction" means only when our "perceptions, opinions, arrogance and obsessions" blocking the passage to *Tao* are removed, and the *state of inaction* is reached. Tao means undoing the obstacles we create to our own happiness, much of what is a set of learned behaviors that are not in accordance with nature's design.

I am not saying that we should focus on the study of *Tao* and ignoring knowledge. All achievements are established through persistent study, practice, and reflection. Neither of them can be dispensed with. After going through this process of engaging with *Tao*, the mind is pliable and energetic; it feels "lit up" by an awakening.

That's when true understanding of our connection to the *Tao* is revealed.

24. Letting Life Flourish

Recently I have been busy taking photos for illustrations for the forthcoming book *Autumn Dialogues*. I have shared photos I like on WeChat. Seeing them, someone commented: "Ms. Ma, you look different from many people I know who practice Taoism; they often wear long gowns."

To be in the public eye is to learn to accept criticism and well-meaning comments on a daily basis. To me, this question raises the issue of being confined by formalities, and obsessed with an external image.

Think about your favorite films. Heroes striving for a great cause often appear to be handsome or beautiful. Why? Because their inner resolve and courage makes them beautiful. How many times have we seen a character on the screen who was outwardly beautiful, but played a malevolent character? They never seemed attractive. As a matter of fact, they began to look as hateful as the emotions they played. By the end of the show, did you ignore their formal beauty altogether and see only their deeds and the quality of their hearts?

We humans have an inner eye, we can see the beauty that lies beneath good looks. Without that beauty, looks won't last long.

External form not the key issue—it is the degree of a person's intention to benefit others. If so, any dress will be attractive if is mixed with the refinement and cultivation of the wearer.

The dress becomes the person.

The person becomes the dress.

Tao is not a monochrome experience. The universe contains a myriad of color and shape. So cultivation in *Tao* can be gorgeous and vivid. Long gowns are not necessary! *Tao* does not negate or promote the beauty of the world. It does not make rules.

Remember: Emptiness, inclusiveness.

25. A Dream on a Notebook Page

Dreams weigh nothing. They cost nothing. They don't need electricity to be viewed. You don't need approval and signatures.

So often, when we remember of our childhood dreams, we see them clearly, because they were simple and pure.

And then we think of the obstacles we faced later in life as we sought to make them come true. When your dreams meet the world, they begin to take on weight, they need plans, the cooperation of others, they are delayed and compromised. They are no longer an aspiration with their own secret energy.

After childhood, things change.

Dreams come with expense sheet.

The rent bill comes addressed to your dream.

Each day is filled with long hours that revolve around taking your dream from that desk at school into a factory or a movie studio. They become their own journey, no longer so simple. That's when the real test begins.

But stick to your dream.

When people reach a certain age, they realize that surprise and change are not exceptions. They are normal parts of life.

Surprises are predictable—you know they are coming.

I was asked about my dreams as a child and what I would have done if not an entrepreneur.

As a child at school, I sat at my desk and dreamed of being a writer.

The schoolbook's pages were shaped in squares for practicing calligraphy, the art of making Chinese characters.

As you may know, a Chinese "word" is unlike an English word.

Let's take the English word "horse." The letters H-O-R-S-E are not related to an actual horse in any way. It could just as easily be called WEDNESDAY.

In Chinese writing (ideograms), there is a very often direct connection between the character and the thing described: the image created corresponds in some respects to the thing described. Of course, it more complex than that, but we could say that Chinese children tend to be able to grasp the bigger picture quite quickly as they grow up.

Every system has its advantages.

I had to store away my dreams for a time. Life had other plans for me. Since starting in Sichuan, I have worked in different industries and traveled over half the globe. From the squares on the notebook page to half the globe: travel and business have drawn their own shapes on the page of my life.

My dream as a child were idealized—and I can say truthfully I didn't find the career and the highest ideal for which I could devote my life to until I encountered the book of changes while establishing the firm.

My dream of becoming a writer came true in this process.

I seek a valuable and meaningful life. Because of that, my dreams have come in search of me. I did nose them, I lived in such a way that they noticed me.

But it was not easy.

I remember when I was first starting my business in Hainan thirty years ago, my then husband was working on a project with excellent prospects. The product was very popular in foreign markets, but he could not scale the production appropriately due to a shortage of funds. Being a problem solver, I decided we should acquire funding. But where? The banks? My husband said: "How naive you are! We can never get any money from them without a previous relationship."

But I would not be restrained by any such difficulties. How could we know what would happen if we didn't give it a try? I encouraged all employees to borrow money from banks, promising that whoever got the loan successfully would be rewarded. I also kept visiting banks with my accountant/cashier.

After visiting almost all banks in Haikou, I walked into the last one with my last hope. It was the Construction Bank of China, close to our company. I asked a staff member how I could meet the head of the bank, and I was told: He starts working at 8:30, you can wait for him in his reception room at 8:00. When he came in, I rushed to him, introduced myself and explained why I was there. Maybe our project was truly good, or maybe I managed to touch him with my sincerity, but I got 800,000 RMB. That was a huge amount!

Where there is a will, there is a way.

As long as we hold to our dreams and aspirations; as long as we focus on what we are best at, we will eventually succeed. The extent of the will directly determines the result.

Due to limited knowledge and experience, maybe we all need to keep trying over and over, because nobody can achieve success with just the first try. But in this world, no path is walked in vain. If there is light in the heart, each step we take will be an illustration of a dream thousands of miles away.

Dreams grow in stages. Each achievement creates new opportunities, which lead to others. The way to fulfill our dream is to follow them as they develop and grow.

If you possess perseverance and confidence, you will believe that this "something" must be done, no matter how great the cost.

You don't need to fear age. Dreams in your heart will keep the passion burning. My dream of being a writer—and also a costume designer—continue to grow, even now.

26. He Drew the Attention of the Whole World

On January 8, 2019, the 43rd anniversary of Premier Zhou's death, the "Exhibition of Precious things in Memory of Premier Zhou Enlai" was held in Wuhan.

As the original sponsor experienced coordination issues, our company was honored to sponsor the event, which allowed me to gain a deeper understanding of Premier Zhou.

To the Chinese, the spiritual core is Serving the People. Premier Zhou represents that spiritual core. He was a man recognized as great by the world. Premier Zhou's personal ethics and charm, as well as his kindness and ideals, still shine through the years.

He is one of our nation's most respected and beloved leaders. His name was planted in my young heart since elementary school and I grew up with the teachings and inspirational deeds of such heroes of the nation.

When I was young, I did not attend elementary school. Usually, when a child is seven years old, she enters the first grade. I was an exception. During "the Cultural Revolution," the class struggle was very fierce. All schools were canceled and the doors were closed. On top of it, my family of four had no regular place to live. This postponed my entrance into any school. When I was 11 years old, schools were re-opened, and my mother took me to the primary school to enroll. An 11-

year-old girl should be in fourth grade in elementary school, but I was very embarrassed to be in Grade Three. More embarrassed was that I missed the entire first three years of learning and my parents never bothered to teach me how to read and write at home! There I was in Grade Four. I couldn't read, couldn't spell, couldn't count—I felt like an idiot. In those days, that I could stay behind to study in the school was a miracle, which created. How? I was able to recite Chairman Mao's "Three constantly read article," with one single theme—serve the people. And I could stay and sing the theme song in "White Haired Girl" in the school play. , True, I could not read it, but I could recite it.

My primary school years passed in a haze. I had not learned to write in elementary school, and I misspelled words all the time. My father gave me the nickname "Misnomer."

That was my real childhood.

Buddhists say that the present moment is the future. Today's actions determine the future. Every experience in life alternates between gains and losses. Although I had lost a` basic knowledge of education, Chairman Mao's "Three Constantly Read Articles" planted seeds in my soul.

1) "Serve the People" commemorates Zhang Side, who died for the benefit of the people. Chairman Mao quoted Si Maqian's famous saying, "Man is born to die, whether his death is heavier than Mount Tai, or lighter than a feather."

2) "A Foolish Old Man Who Moved the Mountains": The Foolish Old Man dug up the mountain with the idea that he and his children would never stop, one generation after the other. "To make up your mind, not to fear sacrifice; to eliminate all difficulties, to fight for victory!" His spirit touched the Heavens, and God sent the immortals to move the two mountains.

3) "In Memory of Dr. Norman Bethune": A doctor in his fifties traveled thousands of miles from Canada to China for the sake of the Chinese people's liberation. He wrote a spiritual hymn "Be not Selfish, Be for the People." This hymn has influenced generations.

This was the spiritual center inherited by me. The thinking it instilled in me—to act without self-interest—is the same thinking that created a great nation—China.

The exhibition was divided into four parts, "Zhao-*Virtue*," "Gong-*Public Service*," "Qing-*Frugality*" and "Ai-*Love*." There was a total of close to 300 exhibits, mostly literature, calligraphic works, paintings, inscriptions, photographs, and interviews excerpts, many of which were the original copies.

The originals came from such artistic masters as Ba Jin, Cao Yu, Zhao Puchu, and Guan Shan, as well as items from international personalities such as Sihanouk, Kissinger and Ikeda Daisaku. What attracted me the most, however, was the famous photo of the premier sitting on the sofa original photo of *Zhou Enlai in Contemplation* taken by photographer Giorgio Lodi, inscribed to the relatives of Zhou Enlai. In it, the premier appears skinny and withered, with age pigments all over his hands and face.

His eyes remain firm, calm.

In his entire life, whether during the conflict before 1949, or the complicated situation after liberation, Premier Zhou followed the principles set forth in Tao: he sought ways to improve other people's lives; he dedicated himself to the public, shouldered a great weight and sacrificed himself for his country. He fully demonstrated the meaning of "those selfless are bright, and those without materials are fair." Up to the last moments of his life, Premiere Zhou concerned himself with matters pertaining to the welfare of others.

Premier Zhou did not leave behind any personal wealth. His ashes were scattered in the mountains.

The member states of the United Nations hoisted their flags at half-mast in salute. It was a silent recognition of that very real personal charm and a genuine love of people.

The wealth he left behind was a public wealth—for the world.

At the exhibition, a song, *You Are a Person Like This*, said everything:

"I can't help thinking and can't help asking / how heavy your heart must be / and how deep your love must be, / that you have hidden all the hurt in yourself / and return all your life to the world."

He was witty and intelligent. At the Republic's founding ceremony, Premier Zhou once said, "We don't have enough planes—let's fly them twice."

Seventy years later, China has become a strong, prosperous country, and we will never need to fly our planes twice again.

Premiere Zhou, you can rest in peace now, for this country thrives as you wished it to.

We learn from the past in the present.

In a wealthy country and in a peaceful age, it is easy for us to take for granted what we have and to assume that it always existed so.

We are blessed because people with lofty ideals sacrificed their lives for that happiness.

People forget—because they don't remember.

I hope our children will engrave the lessons of such great lives in their hearts.

Exhibitions are important because they bring people to life for a new generation to appreciate. They ensure that a great person's sacrifices will live on, just as the effects of their good works reverberate throughout China today.

If the benefits still exist—so should the memory and gratitude.

An exhibition is a sign of both.

These kinds of exhibitions should always be held. The purpose in studying history is to understand the present and the future.

And this is exactly what transpired:

At the exhibition site, a post-90s young visitor said: "What a pity that I wasn't here when you were here; how lucky, when I am here, that you are still here."

Wasn't that our aspiration in sponsoring this exhibition?

I was so thankful to hear these words.

27. Qiming Star in the Morning, Changgeng Star in the Evening

The brightest star in the night sky shines in the east at dawn. It is called the Qiming Star (Harbinger). As its name implies, it heralds the approaching light and heat during the darkest period, just before dawn. In the evening, when dark and cold is about to shroud the world, the Changgeng Star shines in the west.

It shows the way.

It is five o'clock in the morning, before the light of the sky appears. I took the elevator to the top of a 50-story building. My footsteps echoed in the building. This scene was similar to the logo in WeChat—a person looking at the Earth. I was standing alone on the Earth. I seemed to hear the voice of the universe. I seemed to see the ownership of my soul. I couldn't help but repeat a mantra in my heart: "The Mahabana Prajnaparam, the Maha Prajnaparam..."

"Maha" has a broad meaning. It is like a void, without length, joy or sorrow; nothing more than nothingness. There is no good, no evil. There is no beginning, no end.

This is the realm of the void.

The sun rises in the east and goes down in the west; light and dark alternate. The darkness comes after light, and light after darkness. There is form and nothingness, color and emptiness, moving and stasis, crooked and straight. A wise man will take a way between non-darkness and non-brightness.

The wise people all know Prajna, but the confused cannot realize it yet. The foolish and the clever create no distinction in the Buddha's sight. The difference is only fascination and enlightenment. Leaving confusion and entering enlightenment, you are free.

Those who have faith are foolish and ignorant, and those who do not believe are studious. Neither is desirable. What is the Buddha? The Buddha is the enlightened person. The Buddha is synonymous with morality, compassion, and wisdom.

We are born with a cry: we begin our journey in this world. We gain self-awareness and learn to think. We grow and face doubts and confusion. Who am I? Where did I come from? Where am I going? *Why* am I alive? Do I control my own destiny?

As a sensitive and precocious girl, I looked up into the starry night and hoped that the brightest star would solve my doubts.

At that time, Western culture was popular, and I immersed myself in the Western classics of philosophy: Socrates, Plato, Hegel, Aristotle, Rousseau, and others. I read day and night, absorbing those eccentric and incisive opinions, seeking answers.

Over two thousand years after the *Tao Te Ching*, the Greek philosopher Socrates believed justice, beauty, courage, and honesty were unchanging qualities, and that citizens should show allegiance to the law. He searched for a universal truth. He never wrote anything down. He said, "The unexamined life is not worth living." Plato, who lived around the same time, wrote that the world we see with our senses is a poor copy of a much purer place. He did not trust the senses to reveal the true nature of things. For him, the soul had its own, separate reality. The German philosopher Hegel wrote beautifully about music, poetry, architecture, and painting.

But the more I read, the more confused I became. Not a single theory, school or thought—not a single person—could fundamentally explain the secret of the universe and the meaning of life.

On August 8, 1988, I left the factory in my hometown. I crossed the Hainan Strait with one hundred thousand other young people and began the pursuit of a dream. On the deck of that ship, I firmly believed that I would brave the winds ahead of me.

Surely my dreams would come true—in a new place.

I experienced glorious moments, I made a lot of money in a short time, and I spent even more. But in the end, I was down and out. Ambitious as I was, I was forced to accommodate the gap between the ideal and the real. I read a lot, and I was continually active—but little went right in my life.

Not in my marriage, my career, my sense of purpose.

Life continued in that way until by chance I encountered the *Tao Te Ching*.

As I read, a vast world, illuminated by light, unfolded in front of me. All the answers I had been seeking—about my career, about life and the universe—were contained in it.

I read about the great emptiness at the origin of things. How important it was to break the chains of the senses, but to keep to the law. To do nothing that violates nature. To value my own effort and progress.

To cultivate all the compassion and the discipline possible.

The Qiming Star and the Changgeng Star started to shine in my life.

It seems to me now that people must be willing to give, to be kind, and to be aware of cause and effect—yet not be chained to their own good deeds.

Meditation can still the mind and make the body more capable.

Regardless of how busy I am, I always stick to my habit of sharing at the morning meeting. No matter how intensively I work, I feel energetic and peaceful. My body and mind remained cool and contented, even though I run many businesses.

28. In the City Palace and at the Country Farm

The classical texts of China and other countries represent a comprehensive manifestation of scholarly wisdom. Their study requires a certain resolve. These texts have formed the path of my education, and yes, my awakening.

In the process of conducting research, scholars require a pure heart. They must have the resolve and temperament to endure loneliness, since what they do entails a rare discipline: to admit neither deception nor affectation into their thought process.

Thanks to their hard work—often a lifelong devotion of meticulous study and research—we now have priceless books to guide us back to an origin through the history of ideas. In using their intellectual landmarks to trace this path, we locate the origin of our own self-awareness, and we allow wisdom and truth to prosper, just as we discover *how* to understand that truth.

When discussing those scholars who possess such a rare pedigree, we should dispense with all prejudice. I used to hear people say: "A theoretical scholar? Well, what does he know about practice and reality?"

As a matter of fact, whether a person is theoretical or practical in his approach, if he has grasped the truth, all methods will lead to the same result.

Let us not label those who are theoretical in orientation—as opposed to practical—as being of lesser wisdom or standing. Both methods deserve our equal respect, because they have pursued a system that eliminates the false and retains the true; they have created a process that permits us to make distinctions with clear minds: in doing so, we learn the precepts of traditional culture in a consistent, systematic manner.

I have observed many scholars take formulations of complex learning and streamline them intellectually—without a loss of meaning—to create clarity in the mind. A reader feels genuine delight in the presence of such accessible levels of wisdom; it is like basking in a spring wind. The efforts of scholars to make the truth available radiates a humanistic warmth and care on their part. In their explanations, they have restricted themselves to the realities presented by human nature.

They have brought the classics within reach of the ordinary person.

It is they who have demonstrated the profound learning and cultivation of High Culture—and the delicate sensibilities that such a gathering of ideas can generate.

But are we to understand that only theoreticians know culture?

Many of us may have read the piece about two migrant workers, possibly a couple, who waited outside a 7-11 store. They hesitated to enter. They worried that the dirt on their shoes might muddy the store and cause inconvenience for others. They may not have been well-educated, but their decision to wait outside reflected a cultivation that included a wide-ranging consideration for others.

Over thousands of years, people on the land have worked hard to create physical artifacts and other cultural elements—not only tangible things such as pavilions, roads, bridges and folk houses, but also the intangible—songs, dance, village rituals and regulations, rules for family life, folk customs, traditional arts, and temple fairs. Rural culture is the origin of Chinese culture. It represents good ground for the cultivation of national qualities, sustaining all Chinese.

Maintaining a preference for practical over theoretical scholarship runs against the essential significance of culture. Culture should be inclusive at its core. It should embrace warmth and kindness among people. It should be reflected in local customs, art and culture, and be equally present in what we recognize as the true, the good and the beautiful. We should show the same regard for those who live in the city as we do for those who live in the country—equally and without prejudice; we should learn from the classics and practice the teachings within; we should benefit from the experience of others and show compassion for others; we should respect life situations different from ours and forgive people their mistakes, while acknowledging their achievements with awards and recognition.

When we put these ideals into practice, we become people of culture.

29. Flowers Blooming like Brocade

An artisan spirit and the wisdom of centuries work their way into the fluid motion of needle and silk. How many times must the needle and thread have crossed paths to create something so splendid as this dress I wore.

I was not half as beautiful as the needlework employed in making it.

Such a delicate dress. Such an enormous investment of time and focus.

I shared my feelings with friends on *WeChat.*

The dress is called *Flowers Blooming like Brocade,* and was created by the designer, Ms. Zhong Yan. I wore it for the first time at our annual conference in 2017; later I took it with me on my visit to Japan and America. I wanted to show my friends in other countries the exquisite beauty and charm inherent in Oriental fashion.

The subtlety in design and its execution in the needlework represents an entire culture at work. It is important to show the West how closely our culture can integrate with a garment.

The designer had a vision of an ocean of flowers.

She tried several approaches. All elements of embroidery bring their own special significance. The size, the shape and even the luster of each petal needs to be considered. For that effect, Ms. Zhong drew hundreds of preparatory sketches, continually revising and altering the design. Even the final stages of modification required several months of intricate work before the design and the artist's vision became a match.

A designer immerses herself in the material facets of culture; she is mindful of the details in everyday life and absorbs inspiration from them, such as the carved patterns on furniture or the terraced angle of buildings, or the end-patterns on a table.

A dress is a history. Inside the history are all the invisible artisans who worked through the centuries to pass on the techniques and the vision to keep such skill and artistry alive.

An art must be practiced to survive.

Ms. Yan shared the following thought with me:

"Chinese culture represents an infinite inspiration for costume design. As Chinese, we should have a clear conception of what's intrinsic to our nature and make it real."

This practice of wearing one's own culture finds a deep echo in me.

It is important to demonstrate to the West this simple truth:

Chinese design reflects Chinese culture.

All things contain *Tao*, as do clothes created by different nations. She makes clothing that embodies *Tao*. A needle to her is a brush to a painter. The customers who wear her clothes find their spiritual world reflected in them.

At our first meeting, it was obvious that we shared the same frequency in spirit and had the same views about our culture. As a result, we felt like old friends. I am a loyal customer ever since.

The most expensive part in dressmaking is not the material, but time. This designer "tolerates poverty and endures loneliness." Why? She spends several months—as much as half a year—to make one dress, and then to sell that dress to just one person. In most people's eyes, this is not economically practical, but she pays no heed to such sentiment.

TAO gets the work done. She maintains a focus for a long time.

That is precisely the artisan spirit we need in China.

In nature, certain creatures only appear once every several years. Certain roots are buried deep in the ground. Because of their scarcity, they are celebrated. Their appearance marks the passage of time and remind us of how magical existence can be.

In her hands, the beautiful brocade of the Orient is blooming.

30. Running Towards the Future with the World

In November 2017, I visited America on behalf of my company. It was my first trip to America. We were fortunate to have attended a special meeting with President Donald Trump. We were sitting in the front row, and Trump, seeing this, made a remark:

"Americans must learn from the Chinese. As an intelligent and hardworking people, they now have taken the best spots, and we will fall behind if we don't work as hard."

Let's not get into being intelligent and hardworking. *Prompt* and *resolute* are adequate descriptions of me.

In March the following year, we flew again to America for the company's overseas business and to attend a series of cultural exchanges. Originally, we planned to stay for only one week at most, but in the end, we stayed for nearly a month.

It was snowing in America when we arrived; flowers were blooming when we left.

That month's schedule was full of unplanned visits, meetings, and events. The team could rest only for two or three hours each day. Besides, we also had to take care of work in China. That was really an experience, covering two workdays in a single day.

Although my time was consumed for the most part with

my work, I always attended any event that promoted traditional Chinese culture and the *Tao Te Ching* . To my great surprise and delight, I made friends with quite a few good Americans who not only loved Chinese culture and Oriental philosophy but benefited from it. One of them is called Michael. He is a famous international management consultant with McKingsy; another is Sandy, who pioneered the *Smart City* with Boston Group and made it a reality in Korea—the first smart city in the world.

Their stories will have to be told in another book.

Nowadays, there is a passion for things Chinese globally. Be it the result of the economic achievements, or Chinese culture in general, the discovery of China and ancient Chinese civilization has become a trend—almost reflecting a cultural need in the world. I think that Chinese values are silently influencing the world, and that such a momentum constitutes a moment of great significance in the construction of a community with a shared future. This phenomenon has confirmed an aspiration of mine to promote Chinese values, something I began to do several years ago. I want to become an effective ambassador for Chinese culture, and a promoter of global cultural exchanges.

I began my speech in the UN Headquarters by referencing a dream:

"I had a dream ever since I was in high school: to promote the five-thousand-year-old treasure that is Chinese culture. The *Tao Te Ching* is all about truth. It is the sun in my heart I have been chasing and will chase to the end of my life."

I stated further, "The management of my company operates in accordance with the principles of nature. Subordinates work to the design of cooperation and coordination, by which all targets can be met; and once we follow this design, there is nothing that cannot be done."

This is the experience of how culture can be applied to modern business management. I shared this view with my audience in *New York Lounge*.

At the Sino-US Leaders' Summit, I offered the following observation:

"Ancient Chinese culture contains the tools necessary for wise investment policies; and the *Tao Te Ching* can be transformed into actual productivity."

My visit to the US has been an unforgettable experience. Our generation are the fighters and creators of a new age. With courage, a self-innovative spirit, and a sense of responsibility, we pave a new road—a good road—in the transformation from "keeping pace with times" to "leading the times."

Looking into the future, we shall continue to overcome all difficulties on our way, and, in the spirit of the old Chinese saying, start the journey of a thousand miles with the first step.

In this spirit, we run towards the future with the world.

31. Belief versus Prayer

I have been asked the following question more than once: "If belief in things makes things happen, why does Buddha never grant what I ask?"

When I was young and lacked common sense, I used to go to temples whenever I experienced suffering. I thought that the Buddha would help me with my troubles if I prayed devoutly enough.

Looking back now, it all seems ridiculous.

If fame and fortune is the intention, people will weigh every decision at every turn in terms of how it benefits their career. In their personal lives, people hope for love and happiness. Added to that, things constantly change according to our perceptions at any given moment.

When things go badly, we reflect on how we can change the result instead of changing the cause.

Religion becomes a kind of last resort after everything else fails. But it won't help anybody escape the cycle of cause and effect.

Only a change in thinking can do that.

How can kneeling and bowing be of any help?

In most cases, our own thoughts and deeds have created the problem.. That is why I say: "What you wanted didn't happen. Find the cause in you."

Because the problem came from you.

If you drop something on the dark side of the street, will

you search on the other side just because it has a streetlamp? You get a flashlight. You search in the place you lost it.

Look inside and locate the reason why you have failed.

In an issue of *Harvard Health Publishing*, a doctor observes how "our mind can be a powerful healing tool when given the chance." The placebo effect [which stimulates healing] has been acknowledged in medical history. It is a beneficial effect produced by a substance, but not a result of the substance itself.

"It's about creating a stronger connection between the brain and body and how they work together," according to a professor at a Harvard-affiliated medical center.

In other words, belief has an effect.

Attitude, determination, focus—they all make a difference in how the future unfolds.

We have lost the ability to quieten the mind.

Because of the vast distractions facing everyone, we end up expending a great amount of effort to get anything done. Inevitably, failures will occur, making it more difficult to believe that you will succeed in the future. You burden yourself with a self-fulfilling prophesy: *I will not succeed.*

That is a guarantee that you will not succeed.

Belief *can* make a thing happen. If we concentrate mind and hearts on one thing, a powerful force is generated within us. *Tao* says that there is nothing that cannot be achieved.

Does a belief in things make them happen? Yes.

Does this work by asking the Buddha? No.

32. Idols Should Possess Positive Qualities. Superstars Should Truly Shine

By their nature, stars shine. They dispel darkness with their radiance. They bring people comfort and hope. Idols are those worshiped by others, who set an example by their knowledge, expertise, strength, and moral compass.

Lately the words *star* and *idol* have fused to mean entertainers only.

Actors and actresses fill the headlines. We no longer talk about those who have attained professional excellence and moral integrity; now a luminary is someone with a huge fan base. Scientists, heroes, and many other great people have been mostly forgotten.

Our own Galaxy, The Milky Way, contains hundreds of millions of stars. It has a bright part where you can see through towards the center on a very dark night. Our eyes are naturally drawn to its mysterious heart, spinning with us in space.

Yet fewer people look up at night.

They consume the false light of computers and tablets. Our sense of natural wonder at the timeless realms of space has been replaced by a few inches on a bright screen. Young people, in particular, have become addicted to any and all entertainment.

Many of these entertainers who embody the desires of others don't have an entry for "morality" in their mental dictionaries. Some take drugs, have multiple affairs, drive under the influence, and break other laws; others lead a dissolute life, disregard regulations they don't like. They act in a manner at odds with what they preach, and they put on airs.

How can these people be called *stars* and *idols*?

Recently, a celebrity broke up with his wife because of an illicit affair. It caused a great deal of public discussion. My biggest concern is the negative influence on high school students. In the age of the Internet, it has become far too easy for teenagers to access information that can impact their mental health, expose them to negative influences, and cause confusion about life choices. Teachers and parents have a duty to provide timely guidance so that young people will not continually be subjected to such influences.

Idols with excellent personal qualities and a sense of a moral standard serve not only as examples to teenagers, they positively influence adults. Actors such as Andy Lau, Tony Leung and Chow Yun-Fat entertain with artistic skill; they attract admirers with a radiance born of positivity. Andy Lau suffered financial difficulties for some time, but that didn't stop him from helping new directors and encouraging the industry; Tony Leung is devoted to his wife; Chow Yun-Fat decided not to have a child because he didn't want his wife to suffer another miscarriage—together, they decided to donate their wealth. This has truly touched us all.

Once again, I'm convinced that it's a wise decision to invest in the movie industry.

In my company, we have spent ten years managing our performance using lessons taught in the classics, while also exercising a moral discipline in everything we do. The time has come for us to be of benefit to more people with our achievements—and this time we will do it in the film industry.

Our mission?

To produce positive movies with stars who exude positive energy, whom we train. In turn, they will help the next generation to broaden its horizons by understanding the kind of idols and stars who truly deserve admiration. Further, they will show how it is possible for a star to live with courage and kindness, shouldering the responsibilities for their actions, and living a life guided by traditional values.

And proud of being Chinese.

If artistically-accomplished stars possess a sense of morality and personal responsibility, they will naturally attract honors—and all the intangibles that come with being public figures. They will actively participate in charities and make contributions to social welfare; they will have a positive influence on the public, including their fans.

These are the idols and stars we are going to cultivate and train. These are the stars who will shine.

And people will watch.

33. Waking from a Dream

Life is a dream—as long as you don't wake up.

The famous folktale *A Golden Millet Dream* describes how a young man journeyed to the capital city to take the Imperial examination. He was in pursuit of an important official position—and a life of relative ease.

Along the way, he grew tired and rested at the home of an old man who was cooking a pot of yellow rice congee.

The old man gave the young scholar a pillow. The young man fell into a dream. In it, he achieved first place in the Imperial examination, married a princess, became prime minister, and enjoyed the company of concubines.

He lived an entire century and bore many descendants.

Though he was reluctant to leave this Earth, his life finally came to an end.

Because of his ethical breaches, including embezzlement, the *Lord of Dark Justice* in the netherworld made him suffer unimaginable pains.

The young man uttered dreadful cries.

Then the old man woke him up because the meal was ready.

In a short dream, a person goes through an entire life, and an afterlife.

What we call *life* is a few moments needed to cook a bowl of rice. This is a folktale, but it relates a great truth. Life is like a dream, from which people are unwilling to wake when it is sweet; as soon as the dream turns sour, people will do anything they can to find a way out—just like the scholar in the story.

People who blindly pursue fame and fortune often have absolutely no idea why, nor what they should do with the money once they have it. Without a purpose, they pursue even more possessions, trapped in an endless circle, suffering unspeakably.

They seek meaning and purpose for their lives. Money has ceased to provide comfort.

When you open your eyes for the first time and experience your full connection to the universe, this so-called "reality" around you is revealed as a temporary illusion.

Tao is independent of being rich or poor. It doesn't care.

You have a choice. Return to *prakriti*: love, joy, and peace.

Return to giving.

Real changes in society come from within individual people. The biggest contribution we can make is to emerge from our illusions and work for the benefit of others.

34. About "Cutting, Abandoning and Parting"

In a society replete with material goods, people eventually must abandon things—even if only to make way for the new.

What is called "cutting, abandoning and parting" is a spiritual process by which the true needs of the heart are discerned after removing what is unnecessary. Key points in this process to avoid being swallowed up in material possessions, the method of abandoning and parting are.

Otherwise, your possessions own you.

I too need to discard things—for instance, clothes that no longer fit me. Sometimes they have become too tight, and I will then alter them and try to make them fit, or I will give them to people who like them; or I donate them.

Some believe that cutting, abandoning and parting requires minimizing material possessions. They own very few articles of clothing; they do without most household items—they may not even use a cup when brushing teeth. In the end, the only thing they might keep is a bed.

Such a lifestyle is not advisable. In my understanding, the essence of this practice is to refrain from impulsive shopping and clear away the jumble we have stored away in our lives. There is no inherent conflict between the pursuit of beauty, a life of quality, and the concept of "cutting, abandoning and parting." If material things are useful, we don't have to live an austere life.

All things contain spirits.

Sometimes a house will echo the character of the people who lived there, especially if they occupied it for a long time. You sense their vibration in the halls and rooms, in the windows, and from the furniture.

Feelings also permeate clothes that are passed. Those who eventually wear them will experience the care and respect with which they were previously handled.

Likewise, our appearance and manners give an impression to the world, in both the workplace and home. Those who have visited my company have noted its unique environment. The office space looks elegant and simple, with tasteful colors and a harmonic arrangement of Yin and Yang in its spatial design. It creates a long-lasting sensation of Chinese aesthetic, which is a profound attraction to the ancient and the modern in a single mood.

Visitors remark on the elegant and dignified Oriental spirit.

My question: How can we create these feelings and cultural experiences if we pursue minimalism for its own sake?

At times, we may find things difficult to locate because we haven't arranged them in a manner conducive to being found.

That truth also applies to the mind. Too many distractions, and we can't see clearly. Our judgments are faulty. We need a process of emptying out unnecessary possessions and obsessions.

Clearing things up is just an external action. The deeper meaning lies in the life choices we make. This is a path of internal excavation and self-cultivation: our conscious and sub-conscious habits. Removing bad habits from your life requires a tight disciple.

As the CEO of a global company, I must "cut, abandon and part" all the time. I must examine my choices continuously, and free myself from superficial and complex distractions.

To move freely—whenever and wherever necessary—requires space.

35. Autumn Dialogues Launching Event

The Little New Year in Chinese Calendar (December 28, 2018), was a clear and bright day—rarely seen in Beijing. On this day, my debut book, *Autumn Dialogues,* was being launched.

Before the event began, I was asked to sign some books—stacks of them. Although people were moving around me, I concentrated on signing the books. The photographer captured the moment with his camera: not only the image, but also a feeling.

Despite this being a long-time dream come true, I was quite stoic.

At the book signing, many knowledgeable guests shared very positive opinions on the book and my company. I was really embarrassed by the praise they showered on me, which I didn't think I deserved. Their kind words served as a catalyst for my future endeavors.

I walked to the stage and said, "Hi"—my usual opening word.

The audience saw half my face because of my height. When I mentioned it, they smiled in understanding.

In all that calmness, the years leading up to that moment paraded in front of my eyes: starting my business in Hainan with its ups and downs; going to Shenzhen, studying the *Tao*

Te Ching without realizing how important it would be later on; and then founding my company with this iconic book as its philosophical foundation.

I had given countless speeches to my company, at Peking University, in Singapore, and at the United Nations. But today, I was talking about *my* book—my *first* book.

It has 81 chapters and took over two years to write. Among other life experiences and observations, the book contains my reflections on company formation and management under the guidance of the *Tao Te Ching*, or *The Book of Virtues*.

The difficulties I had experienced in building the company were quite substantial, and the audience was silent. To me, I had climbed over the mountains and cliffs and had left those obstacles behind. I could talk about that in a calm, steady manner.

The *Tao Te Ching*, or *The Book of Virtues*, is available in many places. Few practice the teachings in the book, even after they have thoroughly read it. But I will spend my life achieving the unity of knowledge and action described in its pages—through practical everyday practice.

For entrepreneurs, absorbing wisdom from Oriental cultures and for the growth and development of their companies and enterprises is an important topic and worth exploring.

The question is, how can Chinese enterprises—and enterprises elsewhere—properly apply these principles in the context of the growth and development of their companies?

How can culture be transformed into productivity?

After I re-started my business under the guiding principle of *Tao*, I experienced an increased resilience in the company to external pressures, and an exponential growth in wealth.

I look forward to sharing that and other personal stories derived from my association with this great book. The *Tao Te*

Ching contains a vast universe of wisdom within its thin bind-
ings. I wrote *Autumn Dialogues* to share some of these experiences.

36. Heroes

The special feature of an anniversary is the reminder that twelve months have passed.

That's why there are so many sayings about anniversaries and so many rituals to mark the event.

Before the annual gala, on November 6, 2018, I was rehearsing my special stage performance of *Tao*, and working on a speech. I had many things to share, but I couldn't find a clear theme. Another year over, and here we were again, standing at a point in time that moved into the past as we moved into the future.

Reading from a script makes me uncomfortable. I prefer to give *impromptu* speeches.

I remember not being sure what to say before speaking at the United Nations, but as I picked up the microphone, the theme "Chasing the Sun in my Heart" came to mind.

Yet I was becoming slightly anxious about the annual gala speech. Several hours before standing in front of 10,000 investors, I was still exploring a topic. As the hairdresser helped me with makeup, I played a song. I heard a clear voice sounding over a beautiful melody: *How long has it been since the last time we cried aloud? / Are we choking down our tiredness? / How can we count the days with an ambiguous future in front? / Will it be a journey of twists and turns, or one of loneliness?*

The words and melody evoked a sympathetic response in me. At that moment, I found the theme of my speech: Heroes.

How do we define *Heroes*?

Those with heroic qualities? Or perhaps the selfless, who fight for the interest of others, regardless of personal hardships?

China has had its heroes in every dynasty.

Yue Fei served the country loyally. Wen Tianxiang chose death before disgrace. Many heroes remained alive in me from my own childhood's films and books: Qiu Shaoyun, Huang Jiguang, Wang Cheng...to name a few.

Some say that this is an age where there are movie idols but no real heroes. They all live in history. However, *Hero* resists a narrow definition, at least to me.

For me, a hero is not solely in possession of a brave heart, but is selfless—to the point of life itself.

On stage, I began by referring to history. I said that in times of war, those who freely gave their lives on the battlefield for their country were heroes; in times of peace, those who strive for justice, and who devote themselves to their work, are heroes.

The list contains giant names written in great chapters of books, and small names invisible to the public. Yet we can see the effects of their efforts wherever we go.

They live ordinary lives with great courage.

In the ten years since the establishment of the company, change is constant. The effort and the loyalty of our colleagues has taken us far. But inheriting the wisdom of our ancestors will be the landmark event in this company's history.

Whether in our daily life or in business, we do not fight over trifles or put profits above all other things, as happens elsewhere. Instead, we have consciously followed the teachings of the *Tao Te Ching*: "The more we sacrifice, the more we gain; the more we give, the more we get." We might suffer losses in the short term; but in the long run, we will gain so much more.

Competition is fiercer with every passing year, and adhering to the teachings of traditional Chinese culture sometimes requires determination, courage, and patience. This is the book that represents our corporate culture, and we have practiced it for many years.

In an age with diverse cultures, the need for a spiritual center has emerged—which is predicted in the *Tao*.

In a certain sense, *hero* might no longer refer to specific individuals but instead indicate a belief in life—in self-sacrifice. An expansive world view lights a spiritual beacon for oneself and others.

These are the core values of our company: selflessness, altruism, dedication, loyalty.

Listen to the words in *Hero*: "There is a hero in everyone's heart / Each person has his own dream. / Keep going and don't look back, / because you are the hero in yourself..."

In a time of peace, who deserves to be called a hero? My answer: Everyone who does his work, no matter what his position.

37. A Butcher Becomes a Buddha the Moment He Drops His Knife

A spiritually impoverished person becomes a Buddha just by putting down his knife; yet good people must surmount numerous difficulties and dangers.

How can this be?

That's one of the questions I was asked at the book-signing conference. What a profound question!

I based my answer on three strands of thought.

First, it is difficult to ascertain a person's nature from a sweeping glance. No one is absolutely good; nor is anyone absolutely bad. We may arrive at a different judgement about the same people based on time spent with them and the perspective taken. Good people sometimes make mistakes, and bad people sometimes do good things. The judgment of *good* or *bad* is subjective. The more complicated a society's structure, the more difficult it can be to distinguish between good and bad and motivation.

Second, the question assumes that difficulties and hardships must be negative events, and that good people should not suffer and instead live without complications. In fact, that's not the case. In many cases, hardship is the result of greed, hatred, arrogance and ignorance, and people must endure such hardships to find their true nature, just as Dante must visit hell to reach heaven. Pleasures last a short time; but hardships make people think. Hardships are difficult to bear, and they motivate us to avoid them in the future.

The difficulties experienced by Monk Xuanzang are not the same difficulties under discussion here. Master Xuanzang went through those hardships, not due to karma, but because becoming a Buddha was his greatest wish. He went on a pilgrimage to deliver all living creatures from torment. Sometimes the greater the aspiration, the more the hardships.

He improved himself step by step and shouldered tough burdens. He survived bouts of temptation. He improved his mind and kept to the right track—the one that led to the destination.

To live a happy life, a criminal needs only to turn over a new leaf, while an ordinary person must seem to make great efforts, because the journey is less obvious. Yet both undergo the same trial, and they attain the same state of mind, a Buddhist mind. No matter which approach is taken, both are bridges to the other shore. Due to varying temperaments and karmas, people's initial motivations will differ.

Nan Huaijin says, "(You) don't even have the courage to pick up a knife because you fear that you may cut your fingers. Those with cleavers in their hands really mean it, they can kill, they have the capacity of devils, they are scoundrels, but as long as they turn over a new leaf and drop their cleavers, of course they can become a Buddha."

In Charles Dicken's *A Christmas Carol*, the miser Scrooge has had a bad night.

In a dream, he has been led by a spirit to view the terrible future he has made for himself and others. When Scrooge wakes, he realizes that he is still alive. He still has time. He immediately decides to become a giver, not a taker. A change of mind is all it takes to change his soul.

I thought about that question of fairness for a long time.

As the saying goes, "The distance between heaven and the hell is just an idea."

From this perspective, there is really no end to the exploration of wisdom; a journey filled with joy and satisfaction.

38. As Virtue Lifts One Foot, Vice Lifts Ten

When I was a child, I watched "model operas" (the entire nation was watching them in the late 60s.) In *The Red Lantern*, Hatoyama, the Japanese devil, and Li Yuhe, the anti-Japanese hero were talking, and it was said: "As virtue lifts one foot, vice lifts ten."

I was confused at that time. Shouldn't it be "As vice lifts one foot, virtue lifts ten?"

Didn't justice always prevail over evil?

I finally came to understand that sentence after I founded my company.

Prior to the establishment of the company, I wondered about the big questions, such as what we should be doing in this world. I believed that we must make a difference and not waste our lives—rather illuminate them.

How do we make our lives shine?

At that time, I believed that a shining existence meant exploring new ideas. Looking back now, the approach I had at that time was lopsided and could have led to all sorts of problems. I faced a troubling impasse.

I studied the Classics while reflecting on the company's growth, solving problems, and extending my network. I reflected on myself, on others, on China, on the world—and the universe. As the company encountered difficulties, my think-ing veered closer to what was true. The writings of the sages helped me to a correct perception and a capacity for judge-ment, which in turn benefitted the company.

One of my friends said that once he began to study the Classics, he decided to do good deeds and to live with a kind disposition. After that, many more difficulties appeared in his life. His experience is reflected in "As virtue lifts one foot, vice lifts ten." Vice always tries to prevail; that's how we keep im-proving ourselves. Vice is like a big mountain. Whenever we think we are close to the peak, it gets higher still, and all we can do is to keep climbing and face the challenge.

In doing so, we become more capable.

For those of us walking on this path, tribulations and hardships are opportunities. We can confront the demons and defeat them. The existence of demons permits us to see kind-ness—and a way to success.

There is no doubt in my mind that achievements bring greater challenges.

Some people say that babies come to the world with a cry that signifies the sickness, aging, worry, sorrow, failed endeav-ors, and parting from loved ones that lies ahead of them.

For ordinary people, the life we lead is a process of facing and overcoming difficulties. It is a process of freeing ourselves from worry.

In work, as in life, those who cause us worry and disap-pointment are the vice that tests us. We face them with a kind and merciful heart, because we understand the meaning of "As virtue lifts one foot, vice lifts ten."

Then virtue lifts another foot, and vice another ten. That is the endless circle we live inside.

It keeps us forging forward into the hardships that lie be-fore us.

39. The Meaning of Good Health

I remember the grandmother who lived in the building where I lived as a child. After my parents moved there, I used to feel lonely in those unfamiliar surroundings. One day, after my parents had left, I stayed home alone, feeling dejected. Suddenly, I heard someone calling my name.

I looked out and saw the grandmother next door smiling at me.

She gave me a biscuit.

From then on, my new environment improved, and I began to fit in. She was eighty years old. She had a kind and tidy appearance about her. She never got angry and worked quietly for her family. Although she was advanced in years, she didn't act in a clumsy manner.

This grandmother became an important part of my childhood memories.

One day, she died as she was making a fire in the kitchen.

After that I cried a lot, and I worried how uncomfortable she must feel there, alone in that dark coffin. There was nothing I could do for her. I felt helpless, considering that she had been so good to me.

When I look back now, I understand that she died peacefully while making a meal for her family. She experienced a natural death.

The second woman was also in her eighties. I met her on a visit to Bama Village, (the famous longevity village in

Guangxi). On the day we met, she was carrying a large bundle of firewood.

She walked quickly past.

I was impressed by her strength and agility. Her diligence touched me. I thought she must have been forced to work at her age, because her life was obviously a hard one.

I withdrew several hundred yuan, because I wanted to help.

Her reaction surprised me. She smiled and firmly refused my offer.

All the old people living in Bama village are just like her.

They raise their children. They work hard throughout their lives, continuing at an age when others would opt for comfort. They are not forced to do so; for them, it's a habit, and they enjoy their work. And that may be the real secret to their long and healthy lives.

The third person on my list was a fashionable, elderly shop assistant whom my colleagues and I met in New York. She provided us with such friendly service: she ran between different floors to get the things we requested. She was so energetic that we almost lost sight of how old she was—90 years! She told us it was her love for life and a passion for serving her customers that kept her young.

Whenever good health is mentioned, I always think of these women.

These three women taught me the meaning of good health. The secret to their longevity lifelong habits of kindness, devotion, industriousness, and an understanding of the value of time and life. They had cheerful dispositions. They weren't trapped in a cycle of greed and constant desire. Their contented hearts, simple practices and kindness had freed them from worry.

Such truths are part of traditional Chinese culture. *The Book of Changes* reads, "As nature's movement is ever vigorous, so must a gentleman ceaselessly strive along; as earth's condition is receptive, a gentleman should regard the exterior world with a broad mind." Confucius says, "Those with virtues must live long, for great virtues come with longevity." The *Tao Te Ching* teaches us: "Color blinds people, sound deafens people, and taste numbs people."

Huangdi Neijing (The Yellow Emperor's Classic of Medicine) says, "If people live empty of worry, true vitality follows."

Not only does traditional Chinese medicine cure diseases, it teaches people to cultivate their virtues—meaning a cultivation of the heart. A troubled heart is the root of disease, and a peaceful heart is a cure.

In our medicine, *heart* includes the heart itself and the emotions, which are related to our experience of happiness and the value in life.

Therefore, it's not really difficult to possess a healthy mind in a healthy body. As with those three women, we can remove anxiety and free ourselves from material desires. We can keep a peaceful mind, cultivate ourselves, try our best to contribute, and to find meaning in our existence.

In this way, we will know the joy of a healthy mind and a healthy body.

40. Beauty

Most people believe that they recognize beauty when they see it, but if asked to define beauty, a thousand people will provide as many different answers.

Whatever gives me pleasant feelings is beauty. The sense of beauty is an emotion that guides me—helps me to live better. I did not receive a complete education and began working at a very young age. However, people in general think that I am elegant and graceful; that I have a good heart and good taste.

I've had a passion for literature, art and music since childhood, which has opened doors to poetry, art, and philosophy. Books healed the raw sentiments and confusions of a young girl. They provided me with a sense of the long journey ahead.

There is beauty in activity.

You'll never experience the beauty of a trail if you don't walk it. All the photographs in the world will not substitute for immersion in nature. The perspective of a walker is always different. Slower pace, less noise, and better able to think.

Beauty exists in our behavior, in good manners; it exists in the way we cherish precious things and our interaction with others, with friends or dignitaries; elegant movements and actions help others feel pleasure; consideration for others in what we do is a very important aspect of beauty in ancient Chinese culture.

I seek out the loveliness in clothes, architecture, space, mountains, culture, love, belief.

The list is long.

I expose myself to them, and I am exposed to the energy that returns.

Maintaining a charming appearance—elegant clothes and makeup—is part of a social etiquette that demonstrates respect for ourselves and for others.

Confucianism, Taoism and Buddhism present a beauty in the imagery and rhythms of language, and traditional Chinese aesthetics have emerged from their harmonious integration. This cultivation is not arrived at through rituals and formal pronouncements, but something deeply rooted in daily life, which has its own aesthetic spirit. A conversation can be beautiful when it registers the pauses in speaking, the carefully chosen words of sensitive people who value words. It can have its own landscape of intuition and the unspoken words that cultured people know lie between the words that are spoken.

Beauty is a kind of salvation. It frees people from worry.

Beauty calms people. It cures people.

Beauty removes bewilderment from our hearts and replaces it with help and comfort.

To cure the heart with beauty, we should practice the art of remaining calm and patient, no matter how complicated the world can become.

Slow down! Look around you. Close your eyes.

Share love and kindness with those you meet in your life, no matter the circumstances of your meeting. The Chinese character for "carefree" has a heart in the lower part, reminding us that we can only be carefree if the heart is at ease.

41. Fighting Spirit

We have witnessed the devastation of tsunamis in 2004 and 2011, the explosions of volcanoes in Italy, the Philippines and Hawaii; and earthquakes that destroy cities.

Before science, we did not fully understand the forces at work that caused such powerful expressions of natural power.

In 1612, John Donne wrote:

"Moving of the earth brings harms and fears,

Men reckon what it did and meant."

When people do not understand something, they will invent reasons.

The astronomers of ancient China understood that an eclipse was caused by the moon coming between the sun and the Earth; before that, an eclipse was seen as the sun being devoured by a dragon.

But nature cannot be controlled. Every year we witness natural disasters. Many are forgotten. In 1883, Krakatoa erupted, causing a sound that circled the world three times and filled the atmosphere with pumice dust; this made the sunsets have a special quality attractive to painters for years afterwards.

An entire tradition in painting—sunsets—was born around this time, showing how nature and art are always closely aligned.

As Lao Tseu says, "Nature is unkind. It treats creation like sacrificial lambs."

To survive, we must rely on ourselves instead of God. The Chinese possess a fighting spirit. It is part of a long heritage.

The reason why we have this spirit of "combating all forces of nature, literally fighting heaven and combating earth" is because we understand *Tao*.

In the early period of civilization, our ancestors placed their survival in the hands of warriors. They did not fear losing, nor did they admit defeat. This spirit lives on in the descendants of the Emperor.

Our fighting spirit is based on unity of man and nature, and our decisions are based on the understanding and application of objective laws. Nature creates not only disasters but also the spring rains—hence the saying in the *Tao Te Ching* that "the way of Heaven is impartial."

We conform to Nature, we respect virtue, and we never accept defeat when nature strikes.

Nature is not aware that it has destroyed a city or an island. It continues as before.

This is a truth of *Tao*.

We see the same determination in the concerted efforts of the Chinese people in fighting the 2020 pandemic. This fighting spirit is a product of our long history, and it shines across successive generations.

In dark moments, we have a choice: to fight together to the end, no matter how powerful the enemy is. We are all fighters.

This spirit may be a matter of genetic inheritance. Many people think that I am a strong woman who copes with difficulties easily. Deep in me, there is courage to pursue and explore, while failure is never an option. That came in part from my ancestors. Qualities are passed down—not just eyes and noses.

That same fighting spirit was tested when I had so many problems starting my business: Why on earth is this pursuit of a dream so difficult? I was tested countless times and tasted defeat over and over; my family and relatives did not understand what I was fighting for. I was lost and exhausted.

Later, after I began to read *The Book of Changes*, I understood the *Tao*, and my situation took a turn for the better. I developed perspective. The phrase, "Reversion is the action of Tao" describes the working of the universe.

Let me take my favorite type of artwork as an example. Colored glazes and Jun porcelain look rather fragile, but they are so much stronger than they appear. To achieve such strength, they must withstand temperatures of over a thousand degrees—after being smashed and ground and blended. We must all undergo such a process of refinement to find who we truly are.

We are forged in adversity.

In my heart, there is always a certain strength, a confidence and stability. I am convinced that I inherited part of it. The other part I nurtured through reading and study.

42. Empty Streets, Starry Sky

In the pandemic, a virus wreaked havoc. The number of infected people kept growing, and rumors spread like wildfires. Fear was rampant all over the country. For a while, the country paused. Nobody knew where we were going. Some were confined to their homes, while others were quarantined far from home; some lost their jobs, some closed their businesses, some had to make do with less. Some collapsed under the pressure of bills, others could not go back to school, and more were unable to return to their former positions. People became infected and faced death alone. Many parted from their loved ones without a goodbye.

Our country faced a dark moment: a war against the virus, the fear, the doubt, in which all people—doctors, nurses, police, civil servants, scientists, so on—became soldiers.

Some worked day and night without rest; some donated goods; some delayed weddings and sacrificed "small love" for "great love; some wore protective clothes and sweated all day yet couldn't stop for a glass of water; some rushed to the front and served as volunteers; some lost their lives.

The streets were empty. It was as if we went back two thousand years to a time when fewer humans walked the earth. It was a rare chance to view emptiness: it was like an eclipse that blocked out the lives of others.

Since fewer artificial lights burned, the night sky became a vast glittering expanse.

A moment of *Tao*: As Earth retreated, Heaven advanced.

We are a nation that has survived for several thousand years fighting against natural disasters, conflict, and famine. We have faced far worse. And when the crisis is over, we will once again have great stories to tell. They will be written in the history of this nation and be told through generations.

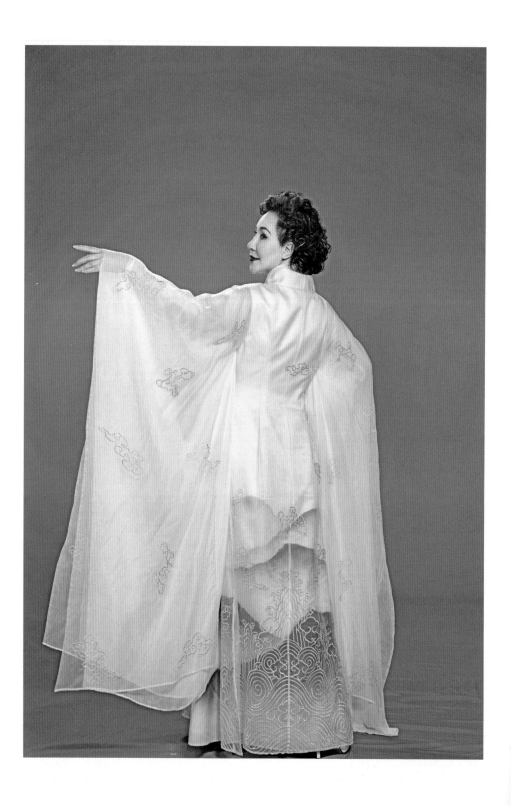

43. Great Virtue and Flimsy Virtue

When I was a child, my friends and I would often promise things to one another; for example, *I'll meet you at your home tomorrow and we'll go to school together*, or *I'll bring you a gift tomorrow*, etc. Children are innocent and forgetful. They forget what they say almost as soon as they say it.

Others cannot forget, even if they try. They are bound to their promises. I was one of the latter.

In the years of planned economy, with material shortages, sweets were a precious commodity for children. My mother once bought sweets and left them at home. I told my friends to come and eat them. This made their eyes shine with excitement. They were so overjoyed. After they arrived at the house, I discovered that the can of sweets stood at the very top of the cabinet.

Standing on a stool, I grabbed the can only to discover how few were left. There wouldn't be any left for my sister and me if I shared them with my friends. But I kept my word. After everyone got one, I had none. I watched them eating and singing, and I was happy.

That was a time when people were simple and kind. No matter how heavy the luggage, we would bring things back for colleagues. Once I bought a sweater when I traveled to Xi'an on business. Seeing it, everyone said it was beautiful and asked me to bring them one next time. When I went back to the shop with my colleagues' money, however, the price of the sweater had gone up. Back then, nobody was well off. I tried to bargain with the shopkeeper, but he wouldn't lower the price. As hard as it was, I bought all the sweaters. To this day, nobody knows that I paid the extra with my own money.

I am unwilling to be indebted to others, even if it means paying for it, and I have been taken to task by family and friends. However, I am grateful for this characteristic. In my eyes, the loss is a gain.

Since the founding of the company, we have stuck to the principle of "selflessness, altruism, dedication and loyalty." For almost years, this principle has guided us. We try to keep the promises we make to others, even if we encounter situations that made it hard for us to do so.

The spirit of self-sacrifice within the company has caused setbacks, but our business has grown steadily into a formidable structure, guided by *The Book of Changes*.

Not all people practice this great teaching.

Our destiny is determined by no one else but ourselves.

Therefore, it is most profitable to live according to the wisdom of our ancestors. Let's stop calculating from a worldly perspective. Acting wholly in one's own self-interest is a most foolish choice, and it only harms us. The altruistic are the smartest; they know how to treat others—with love.

To love yourself, to be happy and have a great future, means being considerate to others. If we manage to achieve something, it is because we are selfless. If we avoid indulging in wishful thinking and give up self-interest, more will benefit, and we will understand more.

Consider the following: "The reason that the universe is everlasting is that it does not live for itself."

44. Planting the *Tao Te Ching*

If you read the *Tao Te Ching* every day, you will gain a deeper understanding and awareness of the world.

The *Tao Te Ching* contains 81 chapters. The first 37 chapters describe the meaning of the *Tao*, and the latter 44 chapters describe the utility of virtue. The core of the *Tao Te Ching* is "Tao comes from Nature." The 81 chapters, taken together describe the role of Taoism in daily life. The *Tao Te Ching* is a masterpiece about living.

But whenever Taoism is mentioned, people naturally think of religion. Today we have a wealth of different beliefs: Buddhism, Taoism, Confucianism, Islam, and Christianity. In my opinion, what is called a religion is the inheritance of a culture and civilization, and the five major religions are a crystallization of human wisdom.

Buddhism is represented by Shakyamuni; Taoism is represented by Laozi; Confucianism is represented by Confucius; Islam is represented by Muhammad, and Christianity is represented by Jesus.

Buddhism teaches that to achieve enlightenment, we must experience the end of physical life and the regeneration of spiritual life. Islam, represented by Muhammad, teaches that if a loving person dies, he will go to Allah. Christianity, represented by Jesus, preaches forgiveness and the rewards of heaven. Confucianism, represented by Confucius, lays out the five qualities that must be developed: benevolence, righteousness, courtesy, wisdom, and faith. It's about this life and its order.

Taoism does not study the problem of death. It studies how to prolong life. This idea can be seen everywhere in the *Tao Te Ching*:

"The heaven and the earth are so grand and eternal that they can live forever, because they are not self-born."

"No name" is the beginning of heaven and earth; and the names "are born of all things."

"Deep virtue is not competent; without competence, ability is unlimited, enough to maintain the country. The foundation of the state can be preserved for a long time."

The Tao is a way to live longer, and with a broader vision. If we follow the example of the heaven and the earth, a company can exist and flourish for a long time, and people live a long time. Therefore, the *Tao Te Ching* is a textbook on the way of Nature on living an extended life; it teaches people how to understand the truth of Nature.

There are companies in the United States which operate according to Christian principles. No one bats an eyelid. Nor should they. Whiles, the culture of the *Tao Te Ching* has shaped the company mind and formed the ethical basis of our corporate identity. While central to Chinese history, this book makes sense of the real world and is applicable everywhere on the planet. That's probably why it has become a global best-seller, surpassing the Bible in sales.

Tao is like a manual for the universe. It outlines the objective existence of the universe and the laws guiding its operation. All nations live on the same planet, and they follow the same objective laws, the laws of *Tao*.

For ten years we have recited the *Tao* with our employees every morning.

The practice of daily reading has a decided effect on the ambition of every person involved. It plants deep ethical and spiritual roots; the deeper the roots, the more profound its influence. That is why we survive the storms and achieve what we do.

Lao Tseu compares *Tao* to water.

Water's shape adopts nature's shape—whether it is a lake or a single drop. In it we see the shape of "no shape" and the image of "no image."

An invisible wind is seen in the leaves it moves. When *Tao* acts upon things, a certain pattern is observed. Its influence on our company is so pervasive that the daily reading is like the ringing of a bell across meadows. It provides a sense of place and purpose; it marks the time of day. Everything in nature follows a pattern, and the morning reading is our pattern.

In the past decade I have felt an energy supporting us, whether in terms of major opportunities for strategic development, or a resilience in the face of challenges. I believe this is the energy and wisdom of the *Tao Te Ching* acting on the company.

It is an enormous power.

I sincerely hope that one day, the world will come to understand these principles. Together we will respect life, be a force for good in society, protect the environment, and live together on a safe, orderly, wealthy planet.

45. Bamboo and Tao

In everyday life, bamboo is a roadside embellishment.

Untidy, weak, inconspicuous. Yet when a typhoon attacks, it stands firm.

There was a live video online that featured a section of bamboo withstanding typhoon winds captured by a security camera. As the storm intensified, it swayed and thrashed, but remained standing. People even gave it a name. When the storm grew far worse and the air turned pink and the wind went beyond 130 mph, the camera broke.

After the typhoon passed, bamboo emerged as a core intact element in the landscape. In some places it was the only thing left standing.

Bamboo was made for storms.

When the super typhoon Mangkhut took aim at Shenzhen, the seaside streets were inundated. Pedestrians rolled along the roads like leaves. Countless trees fell on cars, from overpasses and across roads.

After the storm, office workers trekked through a jungle of debris to get to the office. They looked stunned, because few people understand the power of a storm like that until they get caught in one.

The cleanup efforts took about a week.

The day after the typhoon, I took a walk with Mr. Zhong Yaoguang, a percussion artist and composer from Taiwan. When we walked to Wangtong Road, workers were engaged in clearing up efforts; tree trunks were hauled off, which caused more traffic chaos.

We were in awe of the power of Mangkhut.

From a grassy slope by the road, we watched a grove of bamboo sway, washed by the rain. It looked enlivened, as if its time had come. The garbage trucks were packed with broken trees that had previously looked indestructible: yet they had been snapped like matchsticks in the typhoon. The bamboo, as frail as it looked, was relatively unharmed.

In his seven-character, four-line poem, *Bamboo and Rock*, Zheng Xie writes:

"Between broken rocks / striking my root deep /
I bite the mountain green / and won't let go. /
From whichever direction the winds leap, /
I remain strong, though dealt many a blow."

Bamboo possesses an essential vitality in its makeup. It is flexible but tough. Its ability to adapt becomes apparent whenever it is subjected to stress.

As is said in *Tao*, "Hardness and stiffness are the companions of death. Softness and pliability are the companions of life."

It is almost impossible to destroy.

The *Tao Te Ching* compares this kind of "fragility-with-strength" to water:

"The best of men are like water; water benefits all things and does not compete with them. It dwells in the lowly places that all avoid, wherein it comes near to the Tao. Water is the softest, yet it is the most difficult to damage. One may lash the waves with a knife, but water keeps flowing. When water becomes a flood, nothing stops it."

If we pay a little attention, we find the wisdom of the *Tao Te Ching* reflected in all things.

If we deepen our understanding and recognize *the whole* from the observation of *the part*, we can understand *Tao* and follow it.

We can possess a tenacious strength that meets the test of every endeavor.

We can live like water and bamboo.

46. Greenwich Village, CT

That the *Tao Te Ching* can be converted into productivity has attracted the interest of our friends in America.

Imagine if you held in your hands a small book that has the power, when properly applied, to generate huge returns while allowing for ethical operations.

You would be interested too.

The Book of Changes can be used to create financial benefits, and we are an example of how Oriental wisdom can be applied to real life and the conduct of business.

On June 11, 2018, I began my third visit to the United States to attend the Silicon Dragon New York Summit and the Financial and Investment Forum in Greenwich.

Around the world, certain towns or cities are famous for something. Stratford-upon-Avon hosts the Shakespeare Festival. Munich has its Oktoberfest.

Greenwich Village is a world-famous coastal town. Walking in the streets there feels like wandering in a secluded forest. However, it's not the charming views that have made this place so well known. As a haven of wealth management, Greenwich is home to large hedge funds. It is the destination of choice for those who wish to start one.

You might think that these financial elites creating huge returns must be living an intense, fast-paced life; but they don't. Life in Greenwich, and in America in general, is so much slower than life in China. New York City, in the middle of a busy day, may seem a little empty to a visitor from a large Chinese city.

The financial industry in America is in a more advanced state than China's, and in fact the world is trying to copy the Greenwich model. Cities such as Beijing, Shanghai, Guangzhou, Hangzhou and Chengdu are all developing fund towns similar to Greenwich.

Although a late comer, our group has made some advances.

After several conversations with Bruce McGuire, founder and Chairman of the Greenwich Hedge fund Association, both sides reached an agreement on ways in which we can learn from and cooperate with each other. We can learn from Greenwich's professional management model that trains professional fund managers and promotes dialogue with the international fund community. Our company's successful experience in the field of international hedge fund management can bring new vitality to Greenwich. After all, financial business must be a sustainable business. Short-term gain is not a desirable result.

Sooner or later, *common ground* earns its name—it becomes a neutral place where matters can be conducted while differences are reserved. China and America are currently at loggerheads on certain issues, but I believe in reaching common ground.

We need such places now more than ever.

From the *Tao*, "Each appreciating its own beauty and the beauty of others; as different beauties are compatible, humans attain great harmony."

Although universal in application, *The Book of Changes'* relationship to Chinese history runs deep.

Our company has flourished accordingly. Today, I can stand on the United Nations international stage and promote Chinese concepts and Chinese culture.

47. Use of *I Ching—The Book of Changes*

The renowned scholar Richard Wilhelm, in his *Introduction* to *The Book of Changes* (Princeton University Press) said, "*The Book of Changes* is unquestionably one of the most import books in world literature… and it has occupied the attention of the most eminent scholars of China down to the present day."

In sixty-four hexagrams, *The Book of Changes* symbolizes the constant changes occurring in all things at all times. It is the crystallization of Chinese wisdom.

Confucius wrote, "Everything flows on and on like this rover, without pause, day and night."

The idea of change is not to focus on things but on the unchanging, eternal law governing all changes. In the West, the focus is on things. In the Orient, the focus is on their movement in change. *The Book of Changes* points a way through the constant flux.

At the conclusion of the "Yuanfeng Plan" course at the Zen Tao Business School, students are given a copy of *I Ching* or *The Book of Changes* to encourage interest in further learning.

I would like to share with you some of my initial understanding of *I Ching*.

I Ching is also known as *The Book of Changes*. It is said that over 6,000 years ago, Fuxi, a Chinese cultural ancestor, expressed the relationship between nature and people based on various natural phenomena. About 3,000 years later, King Wen of the Zhou Dynasty, formalized the sixty-four hexagrams. Therefore, *I Ching* is also known as *The Book of Changes*.

After the Zhou Dynasty, Confucius had Yi Zhuan connect the cosmic order and the law of life more closely and emphasize the importance of moral practice. Over a span of 3,500 years, three saints (Fuxi, King Wen, and Confucius) completed this task. Some people claim that *The Book of Changes* is used for divination and fortune-telling; others maintain that it is used to practice medicine, since *The Book of Changes* and traditional Chinese medicine share the same spring; still others say that *The Book of Changes* is the oldest and most all-encompassing of philosophical writings.

A "Fu hexagram" from *The Book of Changes* was found on an unearthed colored bowl in ancient India. The archaeologists who discovered this could not help but wonder if the Indians share a common ancestor with the Chinese? Were their ancestors Chinese?

From ancient civilizations to the modern, *I Ching* is very much present. It is well known that the German mathematician Gottfried Leibniz, one of the inventors of differential and integral calculus, was inspired by *The Book of Changes,* and invented a set of "binary" rules that became the theoretical basis of computer languages. Biologists discovered that the genetic codes of DNA are 64 in number. After these codes were deciphered, it matched precisely the complete sequence of the orders of the sixty-four hexagrams.

Is this a coincidence?

I cannot answer that, but I can marvel at it. And it can be used as a compass that points away from misfortune and to prosperity. It can be precisely positioned. It will operate for all time.

Managing a way through change is not an unfamiliar concept. In the West, the insurance industry seeks to protect people against unwanted change. Some of the biggest businesses thrive on change. Music represents change in so many ways. All the possible notes in so many combinations, played singly or in harmony, soft or hard, expressively or in a mathematical precision.

Mr. Zhong Yaoguang, a concert performer and composer from Taiwan, visited my company in 2018.

Professor Zhong and I share many similarities. We are both Chinese, and traditional culture has influenced us in our work and other pursuits. We share a passion for music. Although I am not a professional in the way that Professor Zhong is, I love to play music on stage.

Professor Zhong says, "High talent" in a person is the "root of wisdom" in Taoism. Such talent emerges from continuous effort, whether in a formal setting or as a self-taught person. I can't agree with him more. I taught myself to compose, write and sing songs. I can retain pitch and sing a song after listening to it one or two times. More surprising, however, was our application of *The Book of Changes* to life.

I often am quoted as saying that culture is an inexhaustible treasure that maintains its value throughout history. I have been long dedicated to the discovery and preservation of traditional Chinese culture and its application to our company's operation and management. It brings us daily benefits.

Professor Zhong has composed music with guidance from *The Book of Changes*. In 1995, he wrote "Composing System of *The Book of Changes*." Music created using this system helps to express fully the qualities of hardness, softness, movement and stillness in the universe, as well as the integration of infinite change and harmony.

With this system, he composed *Thundering upon the Shore,* and *The Waves Roll up a Thousand Heaps of Snow.*

However, he had gradually drifted from the system he had invented until he and I met and talked. Seeing young people in our company with the *Tao Te Ching* in hand, and realizing that we practice and recite the Classic every day, Prof Zhong saw the significance, and believed that we must provide an opportunity for young people to come into contact with the classics.

Our communication has helped Professor Zhong see the value in traditional culture again. He now has a plan to qualify and quantify the experiences he has accumulated and apply the fundamentals of traditional Chinese culture to his creations in the future. In addition, "Composing System of *The Book of Changes*" will be further studied.

After a circle, the path of creation returns to the original aspiration. Recognizing a common experience in the classics has been a most meaningful part of our meeting and our communication.

48. The Great Compassion in the Unity of All Creatures

A few months ago, much was made of the dimming of a giant star called Betelgeuse. Over a period of weeks, it dimmed at an astounding rate, to the extent that scientists wondered if the star was going to go supernova—collapse under the weight of its own gravity and explode.

Betelgeuse is a thousand times bigger than our own sun. People were worried about the possible effects on us.

But they didn't have to worry. If Betelgeuse had exploded, it already happened 247 million years ago. The light is only reaching us now. That is 300,000 kilometers per second for 247 million years.

These are the distances in space. They are beyond our understanding.

We are currently searching for livable planets—those who live in the golden sphere, near a sun, not too hot or cold, with the correct chemical elements necessary for life as we know it. Dozens have been found.

In this vast universe, we have not found another planet with life on it. As a lonely race, we face our problems together—mortality, plagues, environmental pollution, wars, hostility, and so forth. This world is a spatial dimension created by a unified karma caused by everyone on the planet. I agree with the Buddhist conception: "Great compassion (is) in the unity of all creatures." Compassion is a great love and an awareness of *no differentiation*. Put another way, it's the solution to many problems that mankind faces. All creatures with feelings exist in a "total complete unity": you are me, and I am you, there are no differences between us. Creatures big and small deserve our compassion equally.

Today, an employee informed me that many people are now actually killing creatures at the table to eat them "fresh." Most people today eat a diet that consists of animal products. This made me think of karmic power.

Karmic power refers to an invisible force formed by people in the process of performing good or bad actions. This kind of power *involuntarily* leads us to good or bad places. A diet of meat is an evil karma created by killing, which includes indirect killing. Indirect killing refers to the "three clean meats" that we eat. Indirect or direct killing is a cause of bad karma, and it will form a kind of power over time. That invisible force leads us to bad places, and our body's health changes. Certain pathological changes, such as high blood pressure and high cholesterol, quickly follow. In spite of this, killing is a thing that cannot be stopped in the human world. In this life you eat my flesh, and in the afterlife, I eat your flesh. You kill me in this life, and I kill you in the next. Retaliation is not the end of injustice.

The Buddha says that "all things will leave, and karma will follow." The origin of war is related to our previous killing, but many people do not understand it and do not believe it. The ancient sages had already told us that they hear "the swordsman robbers in the world and listen to the sound of the slaughter in the middle of the night."

The fortunes or misfortunes of humanity are all created by humanity. We should recognize the truth about the act of killing, direct or indirect, as soon as possible. For the sake of our physical and mental health, and for the sake of peace in the world: do this: We should try not to eat meat, or to eat less meat.

Aside from "killing karma," there is also prejudice that is another kind of killing. People tend to regard what they observe as the truth; they make judgements based on their individual perspectives. Our worries and other cognitive issues cause the distinctions we make between good or bad, kind or evil—and they are mercurial in nature.

"When the heart rises, so do the Dharma; when the heart vanishes, so are the Dharma." All the discriminations we make are made in the heart. Once the *heart of differentiation* is removed, man will go beyond worry and hatred. The merciful and tenderness will remain. In this lies the promise of fulfilling our dreams in the world.

Every nation has its own cultures, customs and values; but the pursuit of truth, and goodness and the beautiful is a universal desire. As China's President once said in a speech, "Humans differ only in the color of the skin and the languages they speak; and there are differences in charm between civilizations; but there are no superior civilizations or inferior ones. To regard one's own race and civilization as superior to others, and insisting in transforming or even replacing other civilizations, lacks understanding. It is stupid and disastrous. All beautiful things are connected, and nothing can stop people's pursuit of beautiful things."

The building of a community with a shared future for mankind originates from the pursuit of "a unified world" that has always been rooted in our civilization. A narrow-minded obsession with "superior" and "inferior" would never have allowed collective civilization to develop.

Earth is the only planet—and the only world—we live in. We have nothing else to depend on but each other. Financial globalization has turned the world into a global village, and the information age has shrunk the world. As seen during the COVID-19 outbreak, countries and regions are interconnected and co-exist: when one is affected, all are affected. If countries continue to be obsessed with distinctions of superiority and inferiority, and with defeating those we deem different from us, the result will be disastrous for those countries and for mankind.

Whether a relationship between countries or between people, the concept of "great compassion in the unity of all creatures" can make the world a stable, harmonious, and happy place. Everyone has a duty to understand this point. Then we can achieve the great goal together.

49. Tao Born in Quietness; Te (Virtue) Born in Modesty

As the company has grown, I have met all kinds of people. As the saying goes, "Behind an able man there are always other able men." I have discovered that those in high positions and with great achievements are often modest. Modesty results in the constant improvement of virtue, and it helps to broaden the mind, which results in more accomplishments. That is the process that allows a person to acquire a lofty position and make great progress. Without modesty, even if one can temporarily possess material fortune—eventually one loses it.

In the past, I thought that people respected me was because I was an excellent person; later, I discovered it was because that they were excellent people. In my life, great people have taught me that all of us are similar, and that we are specks of dust in the universe. We excel at some things and are poor at others. Everyone can learn something from others; everyone can improve. *Tao* was born in quietness and *Te* was born in modesty. Modesty originates from a respect for all things.

People complain that they are not respected. They may attach too much importance to themselves. They may believe that they deserve to be respected. This attitude reflects only their pride. They may think that they are great, and whatever other people say or do has no value.

It is worth bearing in mind the following: "weakness and ignorance are not the great obstacles of survival. Arrogance is."

There are a lot of cognitive biases at work in humans, and the most terrible among them is *not knowing that we don't know*—while thinking otherwise. That is the biggest obstacle to our progress. Such blindness can drag us into disaster.

Psychology knows that the more narcissistic a person, the greater his estimation of himself at the expense of the truth. Truly great people lean toward modesty: "Great men keep advancing every day, and they will remain safe even if they face harm." If we tread as if on thin ice, we can cultivate our virtues, establish our credibility, and develop our career.

The great poet William Wordsworth once wrote: "Let nature be your teacher." Nature is indeed the best teacher.

Just as water collects in the valley, only when we place ourselves in a lowly position can we absorb wisdom, and thus we become more powerful. Positive energies gather in us. Heaven always blesses the modest ones.

The more modest, the stronger.

The sea is vast because it rejects no rivers. It's the modesty and lowly position of the sea that makes it vast. In Lao Tseu's opinion, people should be as modest as water, and contain all things—sometimes powerful and tempestuous—and at other times, slow and still.

50. From the Family to the Country and from the Country to the Family

Instructor Wen is a special lecturer in "Traditional Chinese Culture and Business Management" and is under contract to the health sector of the company. The 27th-generation descendant of Wen Tianxiang, the patriotic poet of the Southern Song Dynasty, Instructor Wen is engaged every day in a series of public benefit courses with the theme of "patriotism, filial piety, dedication, and inheritance of family traditions and instruction."

His unique method of expression transmits to his audience what he has accumulated over many years of practicing virtue and the unity of knowing. His course is very popular, and venues with a capacity of tens of thousands of people are often overcrowded.

He is a modest and dedicated person. Even when exhausted, whenever the company needs him to do anything, he always responds with the same words: "I will follow your arrangement." As long as the work is connected to Chinese culture, Master Wen employs all his energy. This spirit of "selflessness and altruism" and a character of self-discipline and commitment, have provided him with an amazing ability.

"This is my destiny." A simple yet powerful sentence was all he said during our talk. When the country carries on the historical mission of the rejuvenation of the Chinese nation,

Instructor Wen has dedicated himself to the inheritance and the promotion of Chinese traditional culture for ten years. In a certain way, his experience mirrors the growth in our company.

Before stepping onto this path, Instructor Wen's experiences brought him to meet all kinds of people and to go through his ups and downs. He gained happiness also through suffering. In 2008, he once again reflected on his life—Am I going to spend my life in the pursuit of money? How can I live a valuable life?

Sometimes, suffering is the force that helps us to wake up. Everybody has a different mission in life, and each of us should contribute proactively to our family, society, and country. When we begin thinking about this, we can shoulder more responsibilities.

Once Instructor Wen had "awakened," he re-studied his family tree, family rules, and came to a new understanding of the loyal spirit and noble character of his ancestors. As his studies deepened, he realized that in the past, he had been living mostly for himself. Now was the moment for gratitude to his ancestors and parents, and to serve society and the nation. As a descendant of the Wen clan, Instructor Wen must not let his ancestors and parents down. He must live a meaningful life.

In their family instructions, "loyalty and filial piety" come first, and this has influenced generation after generation of Wen's descendants. Wen Tianxiang, the national patriotic poet, writes: "Everyone dies, let me but leave a loyal heart shining in the pages of history." He then laid down his life for a just cause. As the 27th-generation descendant of the national hero Wen Tianxiang, Instructor Wen has been subtly influenced by family traditions and instructions since childhood.

With such an inheritance, and aspiring to "loyalty and filial piety," Instructor Wen realizes that the spirit of the Chinese nation is reflected in every great ancestor, and it is only the spirit that lasts forever. When we cross time to link with the spirits of our ancestors, we will no longer feel lost in our current lives.

We will live a life full of energy, light, and hope.

The family and the country are one. The family is a smaller country, and the country is a bigger family. Family traditions and rules are not only the epitome of Chinese culture but also a continuance of Chinese civilization. The highest buildings have foundations deep in the ground, while family traditions are the bedrock of a person's values.

I have an understanding of this. My mother was born to a family of scholars engaged in medicine. The family tree in the ancestral temple and the rules in medical books have influenced and shaped me from childhood. For a time, I ignored them because I was engaged in worldly affairs. After waking up to the truth, I realized that this foundation helped me to stand as a solid, beautiful, tall building.

From family to country, and from country to family—this is how Chinese culture is inherited. In Instructor Wen, I see myself. When such people reflect together and encourage each other, they are never alone on this journey.

51. Rules

The poet Wordsworth wrote in the Sonnet form: fourteen lines, each with five syllables. When asked if it was difficult to write under such rules, he replied that the sonnet gave him freedom. The same goes for the miniature haiku.

His idea was that within constraint, true creativity can be released. For him, not counting syllables created a prison for poetic thought.

When I was a child, I once saw a boy with a swagger. I thought this was cool and copied him. My father was startled when he returned home and observed this new walk, and he put a stop to it. For twenty days I had to either walk or stand straight against the wall with twenty books on my head—as models often do. That was the end of the swagger.

My father was strict. We had to follow the rules laid down by our ancestors: standing like a pine, sitting like a bell, and walking like a wind. Today I still follow those rules. This will come across as a bit too strict these days, when people try to be as comfortable as possible.

The rule has a basis in practical life. The breath is controlled by the diaphragm, and walking, sitting, and reclining in an elegant manner not only makes us look good—it's energizing.

Sitting back in the sofa with legs crossed or standing in a slouch harms the body and influences the spirit. If you stand like a pine, sit like a bell, walk like a wind, and if you remember to look up when walking, the effects on posture and well-being will be life-lasting.

Our lives are coded by instructions passed down for centuries, reflected in the smallest details of everyday existence. They had a benign purpose. For instance, we should take up and replace things without haste; if we slam things down, it's careless. When we pass sharp things to another person, such as scissors and knives, the sharp end points to you so that the other person doesn't feel threatened. These rules had survival in mind then, but they still have a purpose today.

When I was in Singapore, I became friends with a very rich, 70-year-old woman who took me to the temple and shared with me the wisdom of Buddhism. She was born wealthy and never needed anything. She said she used to have problems in her life until she came under the influence of Buddhism.

I studied Buddhist culture. The rules in Buddhism are profoundly all-encompassing: treat people kindly, don't commit crime, etc. If we fail to observe these rules, we may get ourselves into trouble—as it was then and as it is now.

Yes, some people see rules as a constraint because they make them feel uncomfortable. What they don't see is that rules reflect *Tao*. Everything in the universe operates under a rule! If we follow the *Tao* we benefit ourselves. We achieve a remarkable freedom.

One final benefit: being aware of how to walk, sit, and recline creates a good impression, and is an excellent career move.

52. Floating Clouds Chasing the Rosy Sunset

When in America on business, I had to deal with business affairs simultaneously in the United States and China at the same time, and it had become quite usual for me to sleep only two to three hours per day. I have always been this way, more or less. Anywhere I go, however, I discover beauty and productivity.

For instance, a few days ago, I was sitting in a car going down Fifth Avenue, and I saw through the window trees with white flowers blooming in different shapes. That was particularly wonderful: the trunks of those trees were full of branches which were laden with white flowers, but without any green leaves to be seen. We asked the driver for the name of the tree. He said, "I don't know. These trees bloom first, then grow leaves."

They flower first, then grow leaves. The pure and elegant white originate from the dust. At this moment, something that I could not comprehend over the years suddenly came to mind: "One Flower, One World." What kind of world does this white flower represent as it blooms on the streets of New York City?

Growing in the soil, the approach and arrival of the right season, the fresh air, the proper temperature, the sunshine, the nourishment of the rain and dew, the city's care, survival in a limited time, and the blooming of the flowers—all these events created such a wonderful view.

"One Flower, One World."

Another time when I visited London, England, I felt rewarded by nature equally, although when I visited New York, it was spring, while it was Autumn when I toured London. I was strolling in Kent Cathedral and Leeds Castle. It was all very picturesque: there were no blossoming flowers, but I did see autumn leaves, both red and white, green and yellow. When the breeze picked up leaves, the flashing motion in the air was as elegant and wonderful as a lightning storm. From flying in the wind to falling in the wind, I saw the sway of the leaves when they flew and the ease with which they fell. Looking at the golden spectacle, I thought that this must be the process of life.

In this world, everything is in circulation, including the yearly rituals we embrace. All life comes from the void, the Great Empty. The leaves of the branches are supported by roots and trunks. The growth of the roots and trunks is nourished by the earth. The fallen leaves will rot and become part of the ground—the starting point and the end point of the leaves' cycle.

The *Tao* is "no growth, no death; no dirt, no stain; no increase, and no decrease."

Endless life, the laws of Nature.

The tree grows in the reincarnations of the four seasons. People walk on the road of good and evil through the journey of life. This is a problem we humans must consider. The quality of life lies in its practice, and practice represents the implementation of thought. The implementation of thought determines our direction. Like the leaves, when the season comes and the wind blows, they will flow freely in the air. When the wind stops, they will fall to the ground.

Here are the lyrics of a popular song: "*The floating clouds in the sky never have a place to rest; and they keep floating and chasing the rosy sunsets. Floating clouds spend their life chasing the rosy sunset, once catching up, it will be ablaze with the colors of the setting sun.*"

My life is very much like floating clouds. Although I have a house to live in, this house is not the measure of where *home* is. All things in the universe keep changing and rotating for given sets of time. They are damaged, they return to emptiness. People live and die. The body, the temporary home of the soul, decays.

The emptiness at the core of the universe is different. It is a vast, lively emptiness.

I see myself as a piece of floating cloud, and I take the boundless sky as my home. I put myself aside. I liberate myself. The clouds change from white to grey or burning red or pink. I have wondered whether a life can experience these different colors of varied experience? I hope that, in floating, I can live a more grounded life: a meaningful, valuable life.

What kind of life is meaningful and valuable? Material success? We have seen street vendors sell barbecues at three or four in the morning; we have watched cleaners sweep the streets at four or five o'clock; we have observed construction workers sleep rough outdoors. Are they living a life without value and meaning? Countless people are burdened by complicated worldly affairs. Whether rich or poor, and no matter what experiences we have chosen for our souls, all creatures float about this universe. We are trying to live a careful life that leads to self-awareness. That is a life with value and meaning.

I keep a younger mindset, like that of teenager. It is a choice, a will to live.

Few understand that "will" is a state of mind. The body resides in a boundless world, the soul lives an existence free from obsessions with right or wrong, good or bad, life and death. After chasing the rosy sunset as a floating cloud, I believe I will eventually rotate into a sky filled with stars, and a moonlight bathing a vast world.

53. Rescuing Exquisiteness

There is a netizen expression, "exquisite poorness." It refers to the pursuit of an exquisite life, even if the price of such an exquisite life is to spend every penny. At the end of the month, nothing is left. They pay in instalments and borrow to fund this lifestyle. Those who pursue "exquisite poorness" eat in upscale restaurants, buy the latest phones, and buy the most expensive skin care products. At the discussion forum of *Autumn Dialogues*, I was asked what I thought of this phenomenon.

That's when I became familiar with the phrase.

This a fake state of existence. The concept of "exquisite" has been abducted by marketing gurus. Don't be kidnapped into a fake way of living.

Living in an exquisite manner is not complicated, nor is it necessarily expensive. A unique understanding and taste, the level of sincere and passionate feeling we have—these can bring exquisiteness into one's life. Ordinary days turn into days of flowers, love, and happiness, and we share them with the world.

I once worked in a subordinate unit of the Ministry of Railways, and the factory was located in a valley deep in the country. Every month when I got paid, I sent a third to my mother. I bought some books and clothes. The valley was not well connected with the outside world: if I missed the bus, I would have to walk and then take a ferry to the town center.

I lived in a simple room, but I tried to make it look pretty and tidy. I made a small dining table by myself, on which I laid a tablecloth and a piece of glass. Flowers picked from the roadside graced the table in a clean glass bottle. After finishing dinner, I drew the curtains and began to read and write.

The life I had led at that time was as simple as a drop of water.

After my failed business attempt in Hainan province, I came to Shenzhen and worked as a therapist in healthcare. My youthful looks and manner of speaking made it difficult for my friends to believe that I was living in a farmer's house.

I certainly wasn't ashamed to live in a farmer's house. I used second-hand furniture to create a warm and elegant atmosphere. In addition to books, the apartment was filled with plants. They were everywhere, on the balcony, in the bedroom and in the living room. The first thing I did every morning was to water them; thus began a refreshing and joyful day.

A girl by the window; a bedsheet laced with flower patterns; the sunlight on fallen leaves. That's a scene I will not forget. It's a pity I wasn't trained as a painter.

Those without spirit will turn a palace into a pigsty. Others turn a small room into a palace.

The shape of our exterior surroundings is determined by the shape of our inner world. A unique world, containing a rich and broad view of the world.

54. Observe the Way of the Heaven and Act Accordingly

I still remember how Typhoon Mangkhut levelled Shenzhen as it barreled through the region. Streets became rivers. Fallen trees turned the city into a primeval forest. Taking a single step seemed impossible.

The typhoon swept away whatever stood in its way: low-quality buildings, those built in the wrong places, those without a strong foundation. People too: the young, the old—everyone.

What had led to the visit of this monster in the first place? Was it because of the reckless damage that human beings had done to this planet?

In China, we have been asked to stop mining. We are returning the rice fields and forests to nature. President Xi has said that "clear waters and lush mountains are as invaluable as gold and silver." Typhoon Mangkhut did us a service: the environment stands in danger because of what we do. Climate change is caused by a change of heart in humans who slash forests and kill rare animals and plunder resources.

Civilization is mirrored by the degree of reverence for the environment that we allow to become dominant in us.

Let's return to the virtue of *Tao*, so that humans will become more human. Heaven more like Heaven.

Soon Typhoon Mangkhuts of the future will remain in an undeveloped state.

People disrespect nature to the point that at a certain level, disasters occur as a consequence. Man and Nature are closely related. If we go on mining for minerals, cutting down forests and hunting creatures in protected areas without constraint, simply for our own comfort, convenience, and enjoyment—then humans will pay dearly.

As the *Tao Te Ching* says: "Heaven arms with love those it (heaven) would not see destroyed." Follow the Tao and return to our pure origins. To reduce the occurrence of disasters, we must begin with our hearts.

What's generally regarded as truth in society are actually pseudo-propositions. Opinions and ideas are often assumed to occupy the same level as knowledge.

The difference between ideas and knowledge is that knowledge—for instance, Science—undergoes a system of trial and error, observation and measurement.

Opinions change with the wind. What people believe is right today may not be right tomorrow.

Truth is an entirely different objective. That's why the *Tao Te Ching* is different. The words have never changed. They will not change in the future.

We need to combine scientific findings with the lessons of *Tao* to help this world heal.

55. Hey, There Are Two Chengdu Girls Here!

Forty years ago, two 20-year-old girls from Chengdu went in different directions in search of their dreams. One went to a foreign country, and the other traveled to the South of China.

Forty years later, Dr. Jeannie Yi and I met again, in America.

We have a lot in common. We both have clear goals in life, and we carry out the decisions we make with drive and passion. We dedicate ourselves to what we believe.

We never give up.

About thirty years ago, a phone rang in a high-rise office in New York City.

With an education in Literature from one of the finest English Departments in America (she majored in the Classics), Dr. Yi was looking for a job in the financial industry. This was Wall Street, and it was a man's profession in those days.

She had applied to a well-known firm, where a single position had been advertised.

The response: total silence.

For one week she had been calling them, asking for an interview. Every day, the phone rang, and every day it was the same Jeannie Yi, calling with the same request.

On that particular day, she reached the company president, Mr. Donald R.

There he was: a voice suspended at the other end of the line. And to him, she was just another invisible voice.

She introduced herself and got straight to the point. No, she did not have a degree in Finance. But if she was able to earn a PhD in literature using analysis/comparison/contrast, why couldn't she solve a business problem using the same methodology?

"I can learn," she said. "Please, give me a chance and hire me. If I don't measure up, fire me."

It was not likely that the company president had many conversations like that before—if ever. Her persistence and clarity of thought impressed him.

She was hired—one person chosen from hundreds of candidates. In a highly-competitive environment, she made an incredibly difficult journey—from a voice to a person to a hire.

The president told her: "We chose you because you are someone who will not accept defeat. What you don't know about business—you can learn. But it is the personality, the can-do attitude. That's why we hired you."

I see myself in Dr. Yi.

In the same way, or perhaps more than me, Dr Yi is a true workaholic. She has told me that all members of her family are like this. Once they are engaged in work, they never feel tired. It hasn't had any negative influence on her health, either. All members of her family have lived long lives. This zone of concentration and dedication is a state of Zen.

As the saying goes, "God helps those who help themselves." If we concentrate on something, without fail we take out as much as we put in, and we will never feel tired, even after prolonged concentration. It is as if time itself has stopped moving.

Athletes refer to it as "the Zone." Once there, everything is different, every movement coordinated, every thought a focused point. The Zone is another word for Zen.

On our journey to career success, and in fulfilling our purpose in life, Dr Yi and I still have the same kind of physical strength and mindset that we had forty years ago when we were young, inexperienced, and full of energy.

After almost four decades in the country, Dr. Yi has dedicated herself to promoting positive communication between China and the United States, and she has made numerous contributions in terms of cultural ties between New York and Chengdu. She was economic advisor and cultural advisor to the City of Chengdu—our birthplace.

Now, Chinese wisdom and a sense of pride have connected us once again.

As a professional who has been "remade" on Wall Street, Dr Yi possesses critical insights into what makes a project succeed, and the qualities required of the people involved. She quickly sees the big picture and makes excellent selections.

In my case, over the course of ten years, my business partners and I have achieved two things under the guiding principle of Chinese wisdom.

First, we have successfully managed our company using *The Book of Virtues*—i.e., using *The Book of Virtues* to solidify our moral foundations and self-discipline. Second, on that basis, through "Moral Regulation" (vs. "greed is good"), we have built a strong multi-billion dollar capital management firm with diversified investments in Health & Agriculture, Travel & Tourism, Entertainment & Media, and Education & Hi-Tech.

In Dr Yi's opinion, our group structure and investment targets are what this world will need in a consumption-driven, post-coronavirus world. Our well-managed investments can truly benefit the United States, China, and the world—with a huge upside potential for world investors.

Just as I appreciate her, she appreciates me.

Dr Yi often says that I am an impactful person, with a boundless energy that makes people desirous and happy to help. She says, "You have no idea how much our American friends wish to collaborate with you!" and "You don't know how much they love you!"

What they have seen in me is, I think, the spiritual essence of our company and a reflection of Chinese culture. That is what I believe attracts them.

As girls from Chengdu, we possess an undaunted spirit that overcomes difficulties. No amount of hardships will deter us from what we have set our minds to do.

From this point on, we will join hands to tell the world another Chinese story: the power of a Chinese brand built through soft power. Unlike China's number one brand, Haier (whose *Made in China* success story was recounted by Dr. Yi in her world-renowned book *The Haier Way*, later made into a Harvard case study), Dr Yi and I will examine an alternative road to success through China's soft power.

We believe that *The Book of Virtues* contains the ultimate "Success DNA" of a corporation—and of businesspeople.

My company, with its unique approach, exemplifies the identifiable building blocks of a sustainable, profitable global company—and one with a conscience. When the book appears, we hope that more people will come to know us and to understand us.

Just as a bright star is easier to see on a dark night, the same constant Chinese wisdom that has guided our brand to a global stature will shine like that star at night.

It will guide those who have become lost on their journey to success.

56. Love Is a Journey of Self-Cultivation

Yesterday, when I was shopping in a supermarket, I overheard a girl talk to her boyfriend.

She was angry. She was loud: "You are not coming to pick me up? Who are you with? You promised to have dinner with me! Why are you changing the plan now? I don't believe it! I don't want to hear this! You just want to hang out with them. Liar!"

Yes, the girl was angry. I saw the anger in her face and the tears in her eyes.

This is a daily occurrence with young lovers nowadays.

To be honest, I experienced the same emotions when I was young.

People love every day, and they suffer every day. Love has become like the campfire of all emotions. Around this campfire, most people sing the same song, a popular song, a song of confusion.

Confusion is indeed an accurate description of love. Why do men and women fall in love? *Why* do we love? Why is love so selfish? These questions have troubled me for a long time.

The body (the vessel that holds life) is the result of reincarnation from many lives. In many reincarnations, desires were generated in us, and therefore we come into the world with different dispositions and emotions.

Desires producing desires in a world where desires multiply. That's asking for trouble.

In such a vast world, and among so many people, why do I love *you*?

The "you" is the result of cause and effect, something accumulated in previous lives that will play out in this world. Love without reason—a cause—doesn't exist on this planet, nor does hatred exist without a reason. All the feelings we have are produced by seeds we have sown in previous lives.

Meeting *him* (or *her*) in this life is no accident. Once we understand these two points, we can find a solution to the problem we face.

Everyone wants to be happy.

Everyone wants to avoid suffering.

The purpose of love is to make each other happy; but in reality, the deeper the love, the deeper the anguish. We love the other person so much that we concentrate all of our attention and support on the other. In the process, we begin to possess and control in the name of love, unaware that we are actually loving ourselves instead of the other person.

We want to control the other.

Love, in general, is a selfish behavior.

We cannot make everyone happy, but we should at least learn to let the person we love live and work with a sense of freedom and joy.

We should learn to be open-mind and to help each other live a happy life, for as long as possible.

57. Noble Men Always Blame Themselves; Lesser People Blame Others

A famous line in the *Tao Te Ching* reads:

"Disaster is the avenue of fortune, and fortune is the concealment for disaster."

This advice is the summary of millions of our ancestors' experiences in countless situations over thousands of years. Regrettably, most people do not understand what those words mean. Nor do they know how great an influence understanding them can exert on our lives.

Enormous numbers of people desire to learn more, to do better, and to fulfill their dreams. But in this world, few people succeed, and even fewer people achieve great things.

Why is this so?

Most likely, those who don't succeed do not have the qualities required for success. The elements necessary for success are rooted in one's cultivation—through culture.

Our ancestors are right to say, "Noble men always blame themselves, and lesser people blame everyone but themselves."

Many have well-defined targets in their lives, and they know what they want. However, they often take the wrong train. They want to go to Beijing, for instance, but they get on the train to Shanghai instead.

In this way, dreams and destinations go in different directions, leading to dismay and regret.

Those who pursue success and those who long for great accomplishments must bear in mind that every good thing is accompanied by a bad thing, and that as every bad thing happens, it is itself a harbinger of success, now one step closer, although it may appear in an unexpected or even unacceptable manner.

These events test our disposition, courage, and capabilities. They test our determination.

Successful people achieve their aims because they keep forging ahead, no matter how many setbacks and difficulties they encounter.

Those who don't succeed, act in just the opposite way. They retreat and give up when faced with hardship.

Success is the result of an arduous "tempering through experience," while failure is the result of not meeting the tests that come our way.

58. A Way of Dressing

Last night, before retiring to bed, I posted three selfies in my WeChat Moments. One of my friends was interested in my home/casual wear and asked what brand I wore. I said, "*Dongmen*-Eastgate."

She replied: "I've never heard of that brand!"

As Chairman of the Board of a Hong Kong-listed company, everything I wear must be a top brand, according to many people. But that's not the case. Some people prefer top brands, but I wear what suits me best.

"Dongmen-Eastgate" refers to the Dongmen Pedestrian Street. It is a wholesale market, where one finds tailored clothes and above-average brand names. My clothes are mostly from there, including leisure/home wear—which I was wearing when I took the selfies.

These garments may be made in a common commercial district, but I wear them if they have been well designed with heart and skill, and they reflect my style in an elegant way. Once, a fashionably dressed girl ran after me, and she offered to buy the pink dress I wore, mistaking it for Chanel!

Make no mistake, I love the top names in fashion. Some bring amazing craftsmanship and represent the soul of culture—an accumulation of centuries that reflects heart and spirit. Any brand that has lasted a long time is likely a crystallization of these qualities.

I hope that those who wear luxurious names in fashion do so because of those qualities, and not just because of the names. I hope that people will appreciate the intrinsic cultural value of clothes that enjoy such love and appreciation throughout the world.

59. A Code of Conduct

I recently heard a parent express concern. He complained that nowadays teachers are often insulted—or even beaten—by students. As a result, teachers are no longer teachers and students are no longer students. If this situation continues, how can we persuade talented people to train as future teachers?

Honoring teachers and respecting the art of teaching has been part of the fine traditions of China. Starting in the Zhou Dynasty, there was a certain etiquette for honoring teachers. When ten-year-old children began schooling, whether in private or public schools, they bowed to their teachers.

Nowadays, students are becoming increasingly arrogant. Teachers can only respond with forbearance. A teacher's aura of dignity, which is an important part of the ethical order of the Chinese nation, has withered and weakened. Because of our rapid economic growth, we enjoy a much-improved educational infrastructure; yet the *process* of education itself is being degraded, like an oasis gradually claimed by a relentless desert.

To transmit knowledge and to cultivate character is a noble profession. It is a vehicle for the future and the hope of this country.

China stands at a special time of transformation. In these years of change, spiritual and cultural cultivation are falling victim to fast growth and a vast consumption of material goods. As a result, society has grown impatient and superficial. Hostility and vanity, snobbish behavior, shallow ideas, and a fast-food mentality have entered the mainstream, with an inevitable influence on our children.

In the process of reforming society and regaining normality, the most important job falls to the teachers. They are the stable link to our sense of decorum and culture in this transitory period.

To avoid a debacle, a clearly definable code of a *teacher's dignity* must be established—quickly.

Teachers have an important role to play in what I now propose: a new *Code of Conduct* where teachers are honored and their teachings respected. As the ancients wrote: "People become teachers because of their profound knowledge and a desire to be an example of great virtue." But according to the old saying, "It takes a good blacksmith to make good steel." Our teachers must be themselves made of good steel, possessing sound moral standards, profound knowledge, and personal charisma. This is a profession that already has strict requirements for proper behavior and a strong work ethic.

Li Gou, a scholar in the Song Dynasty said: "Teachers are not kings; yet they must have the virtue of a King."

In this transitory age, the most important qualities in a teacher are being indifferent to the latest trends and keeping their original aspirations in sight. They should not disregard the *Tao* in pursuit of profit.

In a *Code of Conduct*, teachers must display genuine enthusiasm for what they teach, and they must carry a sense of responsibility. They should praise not only students of fine character who excel, but also students who are obstinate and have fallen behind.

Treat all students fairly, care for them equally, motivate them, and guide them.

If teachers do not possess a spark for ideas, they will never light the fire of wisdom in students. If they do not update their knowledge, they will fall behind the latest advances in their subject matter, and eventually, fall behind their own students.

The key word is *enablement*. By enabling the conditions in which learning occurs, everyone gains. This mode of thinking requires the input and consent of everyone involved.

Performing the duties of a teacher is paramount. Dignity will follow: it is the natural result of being an effective instructor. We all exercise an inner judgment related to our relationships. Using a set of inner scales, students weigh their teacher's ethics, honor and work performance. As Confucius says, "When a ruler's personal conduct is correct, his government is effective without giving orders; if his personal conduct is not correct, even though he may give orders, the orders will not be followed."

To stress *dignity* without adhering to the *qualities* of a teacher is putting the cart before the horse. It is not an automatic "bonus" that comes with the job if you are lazy or ineffective.

Let us hope that soon we will see schools turn into educational communities where people are polite and happy.

Teachers will keep to their prescribed duties, and students will enjoy the learning experience and show respect for those who have chosen this difficult profession.

60. Utilizing Skill

Jack Ma Yun once admitted that one of the mistakes he made was to blindly hire talent. As the company developed, he had to introduce new blood—many professionals and advanced management personnel—to promote the company's growth.

This high-end talent found it difficult to adapt to the Alibaba corporate culture difficult. The result was to hinder business activity, not advance it.

This is a common mistake in management captured by a Chinese saying: "Monks from other temples chant scriptures better, and local sages are known to none."

Monks from other temples seem to have an inherent superiority, and many companies are influenced by this mentality when it comes to hiring people. When a key position is vacant, they spend lots of money hiring a manager from outside. They don't want to believe that a homegrown talent might just be the right fit. Some companies don't want to rely on their own employees—they outsource important projects.

The results aren't always for the best.

If we understand the mental bias inherent in the "local monks" and "foreign monks," we might come to the conclusion that companies have developed an "aesthetic fatigue" that leads to the unknown being favored over the known.

As a result, as able as many local talents are, they cannot carry out their ideas, while the new people are given opportunities.

Some "foreign monks" may indeed be competent and well-trained, but they must face the challenge of adapting to the local environment. As ancient sages also say, "Tangerines are tangerines when they grow in Huainan, but they become oranges when they grow in Huaibei." Tangerines, when transplanted, no longer produce sweet fruit.

The same sometimes goes for management.

The talent Jack Ma hired hadn't grown up in the corporate soil of Alibaba, and their values, outlook on life, as well as their thinking were not compatible with his company. Though talented, they found no hook for their skills.

Years ago, people suggested to me that I should introduce talent from big companies. We invited a senior manager who specialized in HR from a reputable company. In the second interview, I realized that his management philosophy was not compatible with ours, because we were a company with its roots in a traditional Chinese value-system, while he had a deep-rooted management philosophy developed in the West. He was skilled, but those skills would only prove problematic to our company.

Every successful hire has unique reasons for being successful; every successful enterprise has its own operational model and ways of developing talent. As Buddhism teaches, "We tread different paths to the same destination."

A model or concept grown from a different environment cannot be capriciously adopted, otherwise disorder will follow—quickly. Innovation and the introduction of new blood to a company does not automatically mean bringing people from the outside. If a super talent is hired from another company, that person must go through a process of integration into the local ecology.

61. Calmness. Blossom

The Ancient Greeks believed that the past lay in front of us, and the future lay behind. If this seems strange, it makes perfect sense once you hear the explanation.

Since the past has already happened, you can see it; therefore, it is to the front, where the eyes look. The future is unknown and unseen, so it approaches from behind.

To fully inhale and exhale forms a cycle. It mimics so many patterns in nature: the ebb and flow of tides; the earth spinning in and out of the sun's rays, creating day and night; the rain falling and flowing to the sea in rivers before they rise as vapor from the surface to form clouds.

Breathing is what ties us to this world. We have a first and a last breath.

They form a long signature from the beginning to the end of life. Breathing and thinking: are two activities that are with us from the first to the last.

During our respiration of inhaling and exhaling, thoughts arise, appear, and linger until replaced by different thoughts. Countless anxieties and worries run through the mind.

Our brains never stop experiencing thoughts. They are loud and busy, like monkeys in trees. There is not one moment of peace. The more thoughts, the more chaotic the mind, the more anxious we become. Buddhism teaches us that all creatures ceaselessly move in an endless circle of life and death, suffering from constant karma they cannot escape. How many troubles are generated from thoughts!

A suitcase may be heavy when you try to lift it, but after you put it down—it weighs nothing. Thoughts all weigh the same if you can't put them down. They go away in their own time. But the moment we can contain our obsessions and self-interest, all becomes light.

Our mind is a container, and when nothing is inside, the "eye" therefore sees better. Since many problems occur in the past, we can see them before us.

The way to quieten the mind is to take a breath. Let's put down the distracting thoughts and take a breath calmly. With each inhalation and exhalation, we begin anew, like a newborn baby; we move out of the past by breathing. Deep breathing places us in the now.

No senseless worries about the future.

Deep calm liberates us from the blind state in which we are trapped by desire, habit and emotion. Inhaling and exhaling is how we reach emptiness and calmness, where wisdom enters at the moment of "no thoughts."

We become autonomous and unrestrained.

The past does not exist. The future is gone. Instead, we are in the present, the only time that exists. Devotion and love: these will make you shine.

The mind reaches a state of emptiness, a fragrance will rise in the stillness. You resonate with the people and things around you.

Calmness is an answer to questions, a solution to problems. Inhaling and exhaling connect body and mind. In the process of inhaling and exhaling, all veins stretch and contract as we breathe. A vital energy runs through the blood. Diseases are cured.

In the process of inhaling and exhaling, all creatures are equal. The all-important present will not be stolen from us by "a better future." The entire body and mind stay in harmony with the present moment.

62. A Sacred Bird from Antiquity

When I began my business in Shenzhen, the company had some difficulties and I felt lost. I saw no future. One day, while on a flight, I read a piece of news about You Xiaolin, a painter from Chengdu. One of his paintings, Nirvana, had a tremendous effect on me.

I had never seen anyone before representing a Phoenix artistically with the colors, imagery, and atmosphere that he brought to the painting. When I looked at it, the sacred bird looked as if it had flown through a thick mist of time. Its eyes looked as sharp as the edge of a knife. Such a mysterious blue, a passionate red, the bright gold.

Magnificent, gorgeous, mysterious.

Powerful.

As I looked at the sacred bird, I felt the pull of antiquity, which I have always loved, but also a mawkishness over the hardships I was experiencing. At that moment, I shed silent tears.

I made up my mind that, when I could, I was going to collect his paintings.

Seven years ago, I went back to my hometown of Chengdu. My journey was to You Xiaolin. In his studio, we talked a lot. Perhaps because we are both from Sichuan, I had a strong preference for his "Ancient Shu" series.

In those paintings I could see certain elements: the vast universe, primitive ancient eras, the co-existence of gods and humans in a silently flowing time, and the mysterious ancient kingdom of Shu. They weren't just passive elements—they came alive in front of my eyes.

Solemn ceremonies of sacrifice. The rise of the Phoenix from the ashes, resplendent and dazzling. It captured my heart in an instant. I felt as if I were in conversation with it.

I had crossed time to it; or it had crossed time to me.

Since both of us were from Sichuan, we naturally had a resonance with the culture of our hometown.

A brief history:

The ancient Shu culture was the root of Ba-Shu culture, and the ancient Shu civilization was the seminary of the Yangtze River culture. The present culture of the Chengdu Plain was born thanks to the wisdom and originality of the Shu people and their faith in the universe, in nature, and in the sun. They were a unique people.

Mysterious bronze masks, towering bronze trees, stately and exquisite bronze statues. Shocking, amazing, grand, romantic: these are the words Mr. You uses to describe his reaction when he first visited Sanxingdui.

The 5,000-year-old Shu civilization is full of spirit.

The sacred bird could only be born in a place like this.

I can imagine that such a creature had really existed.

Between 4800 and 5000 BC, the Chinese people lacked the concept of the Phoenix. They were aware of a sacred bird.

Our ancestors worshiped the universe, the heaven and the sun, and they hoped that birds could be the messengers between the earth and the heaven, that they could fly like birds, "dwell" with the heavens and explore the future and the mysteries of the universe. The Ancient Shu people had the sacred solar bird as a totem: it demonstrated their curiosity about a universe cloaked in time.

As an artist born here, Mr. You regards it as his duty to

bring this history to life through his paintings—and to ensure that it is not forgotten.

From all his works, I finally collected this series, and the paintings have been hung as a collection so that more people can interact emotionally and spiritually with the life and wisdom and beautiful creations of our ancestors.

Ancient Shu culture, a sacred bird from the remote antiquity: this is where we came from.

Perhaps it is also where we inwardly fly—to our home.

63. Being Cultured and Building the Family

After the second-child policy was introduced in China, some mothers began to live at home full-time. It's hard to take care of children. It's not a job that's well-valued in china. Most mothers are not well supported in both practical and emotional matters. In fact, many experience depression.

When I worked as a doctor of traditional Chinese medicine, I met lots of women in this situation. They came to me because their worth as human beings and mothers was belittled by husbands who indulged themselves elsewhere. Some women had to keep asking their husbands for the money necessary to support the family. Naturally, the stress alone caused emotional disorders and physical health problems.

The emotions a mother experiences will have a far-reaching impact on her children, consciously and subconsciously. A bad relationship between parents can cause irreversible harm to the children.

My suggestion for full-time mothers: if you suffer from a lack of self-esteem and self-confidence, and you are harmed by the relationship you have with your husband, you should study the classics, particularly if your role is seen as washing clothes, preparing meals, helping your spouse and teaching the children. Reading will bring wisdom and confidence.

You will look objectively at yourself, your environment,

and the problems that need to be solved. Reading improves your disposition and taste, in turn creating its own aura of attraction and charm in you.

When a woman can enjoy stable emotions and a strong sense of self, she can manage a family well and help the children grow up healthy. Women should read and study, because it creates a different atmosphere around them and instills a confidence that will have far-reaching effects of its own.

64. The True Sense of Security Is Within

I look outside the window and see clouds floating across the sky. Brushed by the wind, they accumulate and disperse, they grow thicker, and they thin out into strands, a silent music of the wind.

It is not for human ears.

All things constantly change, and we are older with each passing day. The will to reach out and achieve more in our lives is that breeze touching the clouds. It is a silent push to keep moving.

It whispers: *Keep moving*.

Find opportunities to learn, to grow.

The idea of security today for some women is to find a rich husband. It is a natural wish to have. But a woman must also improve her understanding so that she can become that person who deserves her share of happiness laid aside by destiny.

Does finding a house, a car, and a high income, give you a guarantee of security? Not necessarily. People change and life is unpredictable. Companions leave. We say something and it is completely misunderstood. Friends of several years' standing stop talking because of a single remark.

It happens all the time.

Tao tells us that possessions become the possessions of others. The more you try to grab, the higher the possibility of losing it. This is what nature has taught us.

When our sense of calm and happiness no longer depends on external circumstances and other people, we can face that change as calmly as the floating clouds in the sky rearrange their positions in accordance with what is inevitable. With a mindset like this, you will surely have a rich, happy life.

The way to a strong mind is to empty ourselves. The universe holds all things in it because of its emptiness. To be at one with this immense force means doing the same.

True awareness is an empty mind.

If we do our best to maintain the mindset of emptiness, we will gradually decrease the sensations of worry and greed.

I am not referring to the emptiness of a fool. Nor am I referring to the state of mind where a brain cannot function.

This emptiness is minus the "me" in the mind.

If we can learn from the ancient sage's mind and spirit, if we can put aside greed and help others more, we will surely attain to things in life.

Why? Because it is a universal law.

This is a sense of security that nobody can take away.

65. Variations on Solitude

One day I received an important guest. We saw everything eye to eye and talked for a much longer time than we had originally planned. When I returned home, it was quite late and I didn't feel like sleeping. I stood on the balcony. All was quiet at that moment. A gentle wind blew. The night sky looked vast and mysterious, the silent kingdom hid the noise of the day, and melted it in her embrace. A spirit in the sky seemed to be hiding behind the dark shroud, staring quietly at me, and I staring back at her.

I felt fresh and clean in the dark. The night felt as cool as water and I quieted down, and at that moment the fatigue, loneliness and pressures turned into an indescribable, washed sweetness.

I stayed on the balcony for a long time, worried that such a beautiful dreamy mood might break like a dream. I was a child who had returned home. I wanted to play in my mothers' arms for a little longer. The street lamps stood in a silent formation, like a warm invitation. I put on my clothes and went downstairs.

As I walked in the small garden, the things that troubled me during the day became clear. In such a beautiful night, the only thing I wanted was to enjoy a romantic moment of calmness. Such a perfect environment for a conversation with myself and with the universe. And the chorus of frogs grew in response to my joy at this moment in time.

The world looks complicated, with a lot of people crowded into one place, yet it's still a world made of ourselves. Looking back on my life, I seem to prefer solitude. When I was young, I liked to read and write in my warm and elegant tiny room. It was a small room, true; yet my mind traveled to the vast universe from that tiny room. When my friends visited interesting places, I preferred to travel alone, to better feel the depth and joy of it.

Today, I am still the same person. On holidays I don't pass the time with my friends; I prefer to wander around and try to feel, think and learn what there is to feel, think and learn. In Buddhism, there is a sentence, "walking gets us closer to Zen than meditation can." This is how I feel.

As I get older, I have realized that although solitude is an intimate friend of spiritual activity. I enjoy the inner flow that this intimate friend brings. Doesn't the beauty of life lie in being a better person through undergoing change?

Solitude is also a double-edged sword. It can help improve our thinking; if used poorly, it can easily drown us in self-pity. Rumination is definitely not good for our relationships and our mental and physical health.

Let me quote a passage from *In a Lonely Day*, by Romain Rolland:

"When you were with a heavy heart and longed to talk with somebody, he came, but you didn't talk much. Of course, you talked, but he talked about what he wanted to talk, and you began to talk about what you wanted to talk. Finally you gave up, for your conversation had thus become intertwined lines, extending forlornly and powerlessly. You responded perfunctorily and smiled, trying to look as if you were having the most agreeable chat, but inside, you wanted him to leave, so that you could have a quiet moment to gnaw that loneliness that belonged to you."

Rolland wrote this because he experienced it. When I first read this passage many years ago, I developed a response to it and became even more lost and helpless. Fortunately, I came into the world of Chinese culture and sages and classics, which helped me to step on a different path to truth. I learned about softness and mercy, and being more willing to make people happy. Without expecting it, I gained a lot of love and happiness in return

In terms of career development, experiencing a great deal of solitude is not good. We need to commit to others and cooperate with them.

When talking about cooperation, we naturally hope that we are on the same wavelength. But that doesn't happen all the time. When we can't see eye-to-eye with people, we should continue the conversation calmly, and try to reach an agreement.

The longer I practice, the easier it is for me to "have nothing in mind." I listen carefully when I like what I am hearing, and I also listen when I don't like what I'm hearing.

There is a solitary, secret garden in everybody's heart. May we all find who we truly are in this garden, and find the magnificent spiritual flower that belongs only to us. Do not forget that no one is an island, and we all need support and the love of others.

It is a choice.

We can live a meaningful life and also be true to ourselves.

66. The Man and the Lion

It is a face that betrays nothing, staring out from the middle of a desert.

If anything, it is impassive. Those are the hardest faces to read.

Because its look cannot be deciphered, it has attracted artists and adventurers down the centuries.

The Sphinx of ancient Egypt is a mixture of the head of a man and the body of a lion. The head stands for mercy, intelligence and virtue, while the body stands for desire, cruelty and barbarity. Is it a human or animal? Nobody can give a correct answer. Perhaps it implies a structure in humanity. As a wise civilization, maybe ancient Egypt wants to tell us that desire and violence should be restrained by nobler intentions. We are both—we should favor the best one.

We live in a world with a unity of Yin and Yang, the binary of oppositions, where barbarity and divinity, good and evil, light and darkness all co-exist. Humanity is a mixture of all. The mix varies with each person.

The essential difference between humans and animals is not that humans are cultivated by civilization and animals are not. Barbarity and divinity exist in both species. There are humans with extremely base instincts, and animals that show more humanity than humans.

The unity of yin and yang is *Tao*, where yin and yang reach a balance through mutually conditioning the other. To reach a harmony of Yin and Yang, we find a way through the choices.

The humanity of each and every one of us vacillates. We choose the mixture of our own nature.

Sometimes people favor "going back to nature," where everyone is free to live as they wish and become who they wish to be. But we must be careful, because sometimes that leads to a distorted view of the world and unwise decisions; not considering the welfare of others has consequences.

Understanding the pull and push of ancient forces inside us further promotes civilization.

It doesn't matter if we don't become gods, but we must first be humans—and then try to be better humans. Think of the Sphinx. Think of what it has seen in all the time it has been there.

Also think of the age of the *Tao*.

How it has been a companion to us as we struggle with the emotions that rage inside us.

67. Planet Earth Is Sick

I arrived in Beijing at 4pm last Thursday.

As I left the plane, there was a powerful smell of burning wood in the air. I looked around, trying to determine the source of the smell. I looked up at the sky, and it was dark—where there should have been blue and white clouds, I saw floating particles and other impurities caused by omnipresent pollution. I could not help but lament: This is our capital, Beijing!

Smog! In the process of promoting and developing a material lifestyle, human beings have generated vast amounts of pollution, with which we must now live. On the street, countless faces wear masks, and countless cars have air purifiers. People who are wrapped up in the hustle and bustle of the city seem to have accepted that this is a normal state of urban existence.

We must once again understand that humanity is locked inside the Yin /Yang principle that operates in this dimensional space.

As the old saying goes: "Yin and Yang are the truth of the universe." It can be readily observed that all human inventions produce two kinds of results—good and bad.

Yin and Yang represent the two sides of things: the positive and the negative, light and dark, the forceful and the receptive, the full and the empty, the good and the bad. Yin and Yang constantly interact, shifting in strength, rising and falling.

Spears and shields do not exist in isolation. Contradictions coexist containment and release drive the development of things.

The rapid expansion of material needs leads it to invent and innovate in order to continue enjoying the convenience and comfort created by material development.

Little do we realize that in the process of enjoying the senses, we are tasting the bitter fruits of a society that places such a great emphasis on material possession.

What is important is how we apply the principles of Yin and Yang. Here, I cannot help but think of a sentence in Laozi's *Tao Te Ching*: "Blessings and misfortunes come in turn." That is to say, bad things can lead to a favorable result. Good things can lead to adverse results. Blessings and misfortunes often travel together.

In nature, the nettle and the dock leaf frequently grow close to each other.

One stings; the other soothes the pain.

Question here is: where to strike the balance? Human nature is to always want something better and that life is always more convenient. But where to draw the line? When is enough?

From the latter half of 2019 to the spring of 2020, Planet Earth has been visited by multiple disasters. Swine flu, catastrophic wildfires that raged for months in Australia, a plague of locusts in Africa that landed on crops which disappeared in seconds, the COVID-19 pandemic, as well as volcanic eruptions and earthquakes. People are worried. What's going on with our planet? Will things get better?

All creatures on the planet form an integral whole. We belong here, on this planet and in this universe. According to the Butterfly Effect, a slight move in one part may affect the whole world, meaning that we cannot control the myriad changes resulting from a series of causes and effects. We truly have no respect. Destructive mining, excessive development, pollution... all have overwhelmed the planet. Earth is sick. It's trying to cure itself through an adjustment of frequencies.

Our position on the planet's surface is delicate. The consequences for us are potentially devastating.

Ultimately, sickness is a warning. If not cured, it will lead to a greater "fracture." And the definition of cure is to know how to recover, what to do after the recovery and how to avoid making the same mistakes. As I often say, Tao is in everything. Tao is in the universe, in all things in the universe, and in human lives. As humans, the most important thing for us is to act according to *Tao*. The concentrated outbreak of disasters reminds us to return to *Tao*.

In the global pandemic, people have settled at home. Cities have grown quiet at night. Perhaps this is the opportunity for our country to reflect. The ones who are causing such severe damage to the planet can finally walk on the path of *Tao*, which forbids such destruction.

The locusts are not evil. They are living creatures. They want to stay alive.

A virus is not evil. It is a living creature. It wants to stay alive. It does this by spreading from one human to another. Unfortunately, that causes great suffering.

The people who set the wildfires—they are criminals.

The people who cut down rainforests—they are stealing from future generations.

The people who hunt a priceless heritage of ancient life—the Rhino—for greed and lust. They are destroyers.

We will reap what we sow.

Tao is mindless. We will not be able to cope with the forces of nature we unleash by our actions.

We should reflect on our willful massacre of other creatures that upset the ecological balance that made way for the spreading of the virus.

If we all acted according to Tao with regard for other creatures and self-discipline, we can "attain the utmost in passivity and hold firm to the basis of quietude" to reach a state of "original simplicity," we will be healthy and generate wisdom. The planet will recover if given the chance.

In this global pandemic, few of us are qualified to act as first responders. Still, we can do our bit to benefit the family. In the time when we cannot go out, we can revive the art of conversation and do the other things we have put aside. This is what we call "returning home." Each meal warms us together, as if around a campfire. Each plant we grow at home, each bowl and glass, are signs of civilization, which, like time, is a precious thing. We can read and study.

The Earth wants us to provide her with silence and peace. Are we listening?

68. A View to the Future

If social media is "social," then why are more people isolated now than ever before?

So many young people feel that they are going it alone. That's because the technological world has embraced isolation even while it claims togetherness.

The digital world is a reflection of the real world, but it cannot substitute for it. That is why reading is so important. Reading connects us to our heritage and to our traditions. That is vitally important because it teaches self-expression.

Over the past 40 years of engagement with the world, China has made remarkable achievements. Young people will be the main force in the great rejuvenation of the Chinese nation. Some people are not so sure that the post-90s and the millennial generation can shoulder the great responsibility, for many of them have never experienced the hardships their parents have.

Some young people fought against COVID-19, sacrificed their lives in peacekeeping missions, and helped during disasters. They have shown us the power of youth and the spirit of responsibility. Others lived at their parents' house and seemed unaware of the outside world beyond their digital friends.

We use innovation for education, for building character and giving people a sense of purpose.

The President stresses the importance of education. He

places much emphasis on the cultivation of a time-tested value system culture that stresses education. He openly says that young people should "overcome the superficial atmosphere, read more classics, and understand the *whys* and *wherefores.*"

Reading provides this deep layering, the connection of body to the book, mind to the ideas, and both to a tradition.

A digital screen does not.

When I worked as a volunteer, I met young people who were simple, bright, modest and diligent. They demonstrated a consideration for others in the smallest things. They were free of the superficiality that too many young people exhibit.

Every generation bears the burden of handing on inherited wisdoms to the following generation. People born today will live in an age of advanced technologies, blooming cultures and prosperous cities, and they will enjoy the fruits of modern civilization. The *Tao* will be there for them too. I hope they will respect life, keep a peaceful mind, and maintain a propriety in their actions. They may become the most kind-hearted, most cultivated and most creative generation yet.

69. Choice Blooms in the Ordinary

I have heard people lament, "We once dreamed of adventure and achievements," but in the end, their dreams receded into a dull existence.

Others say that an ideal life is about spiritual progress, but we are all trapped by a long list of daily necessities.

Every dream seems to be a compromise with every day.

Life is teeming with distractions, and dreams are far away, it seems. Both your everyday life and your dreams both suffer as a result.

The path we choose is a choice of the heart.

When I was young, I lived alone in the dormitory. I made steamed buns by myself, sawed wood and made my own table. I put a vase of wildflowers on it, placed a book on the table, and began to read, to write to sing. My life at that time was most definitely taken up with daily necessities.

But I saw these other activities as also necessary. Yes, a choice, about what to include in my life, and what to exclude.

I remember those fragrant weeks and months. The dream of being a writer quietly grew because I quietly sustained it. Because of the challenges and hopeless situations I faced then, I kept the writing alive.

Now, several decades later, it has begun to bloom. (I also became a composer and a singer, and built a global company).

My young dreams and ideals were not swamped under a daily life of burning coal, rice, cooking oil and salt.

Those activities helped me. They kept me grounded.

In addition to making tables, clothing, curtains, draperies and cloths, I like to plan and execute meals for a dozen people on my own. This process involves a strategy involving food, heating, music, dish selection, etc. Lao Tseu says, "Rule a kingdom as you would fry shrimp." Isn't this insightful? It takes the same kind of careful preparation and strategic planning. Many great leaders also pursued an active domestic life.

If we become proactive creators instead of passive followers, many things can be balanced. The reason our ideals are sometimes defeated by reality is that we give up

We defeat ourselves first.

And life goes on. Some people become indolent after they get married and have children; they choose to let go of their ambitions, and they no longer pay attention to their appearance. They live on fragmented information from cellphones and gossip.

Long ago, our ancestors showed us how to live an elegant and fulfilling life. Material satisfaction and spiritual satisfaction are both necessary. With our heart in what we do, we make the choices that bloom at a later time.

Face things instead of avoiding avoid them.

Stop drowning yourself in the past or in the future.

Focus on the present moment.

You will then discover your life is as fair as a fine tapestry of golden brocades. Your dreams will never stop.

One day, they will arrive.

The dream and the reality become one.

70. Conquest without Strife

An intangible anxiety seems to be fully in control of people's lives.

I see it on social media and on lifestyle channels, local news, everywhere.

The negativity is non-stop. In fact, negativity has become a commodity, and that commodity sells very well; otherwise it would not be so prevalent.

For publications aimed at young women, here is a gem: "You Are Being Abandoned by Your Peers."

These online publications create uncertainty, fear, and a gnawing sense that you are missing out on something. Whatever you are doing, something much better is happening somewhere else, and all your friends are there.

Complete nonsense—but it sells.

Anxiety and uncertainty are profitable, at least in the short term. These sensational articles cause people enough distress that they lie awake at night. Others worry that they may not have the resources to purchase products being advertised. Rivalry creeps into every moment of the day.

In an age of pervasive online peer pressure and economic growth, society is acting as if everyone is standing at a train station.

Those on the platform worry that they may not get on the train; those on the train worry that they may not get a seat; those sitting in the seats think the seats are not good enough;

those sitting in good seats worry that the seats might be taken away at any time.

In the movie, *The Pursuit of Happyness*, the hero sees a stockbroker going to work in a Ferrari, and he asks why he can't be as happy as that.

Everybody asks this question at some point.

Meanwhile, the pressure to get things is relentless.

Turn on a cellphone—there it is.

A tablet? There it is.

The entire world is one big advertisement.

After living in this environment for a long time, we naturally change our thinking to suit that environment: we now believe it's right to "fight" for things, because if you don't, you'll suffer loss and will look foolish in front of other people.

For some very ambitious people, that means learning to fight better than others.

The mindset has been formed. Now it really begins. Blind hustling for profits has become a common sight in the business world we see today.

Everywhere is a war zone.

The *Tao Te Ching* is familiar with this situation:

The more you fight, the less you get.

In a world of competition, people may find the concept of "conquest without conflict" strange at best. To their way of thinking, in a world of fierce competition, "not fighting" represents a passive position, which will only end in defeat.

A note: When I was young, there weren't such huge gaps between rich and poor, and everyone contributed to society. People interested themselves in ideas and the spiritual life. This was the prevailing mainstream ideology back then. Despite scarcities in material, people were happier.

Indeed, in order to achieve your conquest, avoiding strife is not enough. According to another teaching by Lao Tseu, "water benefits all things and competes with none." In order to conquer, we must "benefit all things." Although water does not compete, yet it's never idle. "In its dwelling, it loves the lowly earth; in its heart, it loves what is profound; in its relations with others, it loves kindness; in its words, it loves sincerity; in government, it loves peace; in business affairs, it loves ability; in its actions, it loves choosing the right time. It is because it does not contend, that it is without reproach," thus water reaches the level of "dwelling in lowly places that all disdain, and benefiting all." When all things can't do without it, it no longer needs to contend. What a triumph!

The same applies in the company management. Those contending for power and profit rarely end up well, while those with core technologies in hand can always find their positions where no one else can replace them. Those who follow the principles of *Tao* have achieved excellent results.

If, like the hero in *The Pursuit of Happyness*, you can take your mind from external influence and distractions. Adjust your way of living. Stop belittling yourself. Everyone has a talent. What is necessary is to find that talent, polish it, and use it to accumulate the benefits over time: "conquest without strife."

71. Encouragement and Charity

We all remember scenes from our school days, perhaps because so much of life lay ahead of us, or that being so young is such an intense time.

Angry words, impatient words, formal words—they come and go—but the time taken when a teacher or a friend says something inspiring?

The power of encouragement is immense. It can literally change a life.

If you live ten centuries, you will never forget those words. You will recall where you were standing when you heard them, what you were wearing, whether it was raining or sunny outside. Your memory will preserve the entire scene because of a few simple words.

Why do we remember encouragement so acutely? Perhaps nature recognizes the importance of encouragement and does what it can to brand it deep into our conscious mind whenever it occurs.

In 1768, the German writer and visionary Goethe said:

"Instruction does much, but encouragement does everything."

If you have ever watched a bird teaching a fledgling to fly, you will see how often the mother flies away and returns. Eventually, the bird takes to the air for the first time, opens its wings, and magically, it stays aloft. The encouragement from the mother is a natural ritual, but the mother will keep to that ritual for as long as she can.

Human encouragement is different. When a spiritual channel exists between people, a person with empathy chooses words that will instill a powerful dream into the heart, or courage when courage is needed.

A friend who stands by your side when others do not? That too is encouragement. That too is never forgotten.

I believe that encouragement can be a form of charity, especially between strangers.

Once someone said to me: "Ms. Ma, it's good of you to give to the needy—you will accumulate good fortune. When I am as rich as you are, I'll do the same."

I immediately thought of two passages in the *Tao Te Ching*: "He lives for other people, and grows richer himself; he gives to other people, and has plenty."

The second: "He who holds it, loses it."

Either way, if this man intends to give nothing until he becomes rich, he will never be rich.

These people fear that giving before they become wealthy will cause them financial harm: their focus is gain and loss.

But the more they focus on gains, the more they lose.

Parsimony is a cause of poverty.

Some help others as the price of doing business, and at the same time, they calculate their gains. There is no merit in helping others for those reasons. Some assist others in an arrogant fashion: *I am helping you and show mercy to you—so you must treat me well in the future.* If that's your mentality, beggars will not feel gratitude. Inside, they will belittle you.

If we help from the bottom of the heart, and with no strings attached, we can experience the true returns of charity. We can also help others in so many more ways than material assistance.

A poor man asks Buddha: "Why am I so poor?"

Buddha answers: "Because you never help poor people."

The poor man then says: "I don't have money, so how can I help others?"

Buddha answers: "Even if you don't have money, you can still help others in many ways: you can smile, spread joy, praise the qualities of others, prayer for them, and respect them. These are all ways of helping others."

This world we live in is a chaotic world. The coexistence of yin and yang means that we live daily with the binary effects of good and bad, kindness and cruelty, dignity and corruption, wealth and poverty.

Empathy for others helps us to create signposts in this chaos. Never underestimate the smile you give; your kind words to a child; that small, kind deed—taking care of plants and animals, whatever it is. All of it is amplified in the world of *Tao*.

Those asking for assistance are the disciples Buddha sent to test us—so that we can be saved from ourselves. As for the highest state of helping others, the Vimalakīrti Sūtra has the answer. If we help those in need because we wish to accumulate future blessings, we are beggars ourselves; but if we see the Buddha within them—and feel grateful—then we will find a way out of the human maze.

It is with gratitude that we help those in need.

Not mercy.

72. Song

Every morning, after reciting the *Tao Te Ching*, we recite the Song of The Great Spirit.

The song radiates positive energy and transmits a vital spirit. It is inspiring. It becomes its own force inside us, we feel it support us as we sing it.

All lives are a form of energy, and we are exposed in different ways to the healing powers of nature. *The Inner Canon of the Yellow Emperor,* the most authoritative text in early medical theory, says: "When *vital energy* exists inside, pathogenic energy cannot invade." It helps the human body to defend itself.

Just as all plants are shaped differently according to their different needs, we should live our lives splendidly and lively in different ways. If you were a plant, Would you live by the window or outside? Light or dark? Chilly or warm? We are all nourished by the sun and moved by the wind.

We live in a garden, both humans and the creatures of Earth. We are related to each other more than we could ever believe.

When we sing together, we invoke energy.

In a chorus, the voice becomes resonant, the posture straight, the mood elevated.

We experience a passion for the day ahead. A dynamic feeling flows through us and is projected outward in frequencies of sound.

In nature's morning ritual, two events occur at the same time: a gathering and a song.

When we stand in a hall in the light of morning, we experience a powerful force in nature: the chorus. Go outside at dawn or nightfall and you will hear a chorus of birds or tree-frogs filling the air with song. Nothing connects us more to the spiritual channels of nature than song.

Being in a large group allows those who may feel uncertain to give full voice to the song. It is hardwired into the faculties and the nervous system. Gradually, there is less reliance on memory and more emphasis on emotion and purpose. There is no room for worry or unhappiness: the song in itself and the act of singing reinforces a positive outlook. We take on the qualities of what is sung.

The great poet WB Yeats wrote, *"How can we know the dancer from the dance?"*

The things we do every day tend to have a higher function in life. For one thing, repetition allows us to master techniques that would be impossible if only practiced a couple of times.

A master chef does not become an expert in three months. Every day, for hours, the chef practices the culinary arts. When he serves a quick lunch to some guests, one of them might say, "Well that was quick—it only took you twenty minutes." But it took the chef twenty years to acquire those skills. The time behind the time cannot be seen.

Humans adopt all manner of rituals as part of daily life: The daily practice of a concert pianist, the daily reading of a book, the meals we eat together, all these create pathways in the brain and a sense of contentment in the heart.

Even at a distance, spirit and song can protect us.

In his *Song of Great Spirit*, Wen Tianxiang recounts that, although he was captured after a defeat and thrown into a dreadful prison, diseases could not harm him because of a spirit that gave him the courage to face his destiny. In this age, we don't need to sacrifice our lives for a just cause, as Hero Wen did, but we should be aware of the Great Spirit inside us to preserve our health and develop our awareness.

In ancient Chinese medicine, the scarcity of the Great Spirit is regarded as the root of disease. Its presence in a person's attitude toward life makes it difficult for bad energy to penetrate the system.

Notice how frequently people with poor dispositions become ill.

Vitality is immunity.

In singing the Song of the Great Spirit, we connect ourselves to the power of *Tao*.

Yin and Yang are in ceaseless transformation.

The ritual supports the efforts we make to face challenges in the day ahead.

We are getting better at solving problems; hence, we will be better prepared to meet future challenges.

Everything is practice.

Nature values repetition. How many times have you seen a sunset? There is one every single day.

And so we sing every single day.

73. Setbacks

Not all people get what they wish for.

They are a bastion of ambition in the beginning, but in time they fall prey to various anxieties, and end up accomplishing nothing. They resign themselves to secondary choices. They hope at least for an uncomplicated life. But even those lesser choices come with worry, because the person who made those choices is the same one who gave up on the first choice.

People ask why this is. Why are they being placed in these situations? How do we eliminate distraction? This is difficult. Whatever we see, hear, smell, taste, and touch, adds to the influence external things exert on our attention. We tramp along to unfulfilled lives.

Wrong concepts torture us, we progress slower, we grow tired. Each step we take drags us down. Eventually we want to give up and trudge along indifferently.

Buddhism describes as *obstacles* the state of suffering that deprives people of awareness. It is not the mountain in the distance but the grit in our shoes that holds us back. The grit is an obstacle, or distracting thoughts, created by our view of the world. Whatever happens in the outside world is a mirror of the mind itself. Clear the obstacles on the inside, and the obstacles outside will vanish.

Obstacles exist in business life as much as in the personal.

I've been asked: "When will people stop attacking our company?"

My response to that question is not to even think about it. *Tao* is generated by Yin and Yang, and it is unrealistic to expect that all things will proceed in a manner always pleasing to us. In fact, that would not be desirable. The co-existence of Yin and Yang, and all the opposites that form in nature, is what drives our company forward.

We should not expect others to approve of us completely; our company practices Tao as an active philosophy, and seeking unanimous approval is not how *Tao* works, nor would it conform to the realities of Yin and Yang—in this case, the cyclical movement of sustainable development.

Conflict is normal; the key is how to steer a path through the changes.

We can stop resisting what resists us; we can avoid fighting back against setbacks. Instead we can convert that energy into acceptance, and gratitude for the opportunities we have been given. This mindset enables our cells to receive the light of energy. We devote ourselves completely to our activities and feel joy from the inside out. We waste no time worrying about personal "gains" and "losses" and focus on achieving a fulfilling life, which is the ultimate gain. Nothing will benefit our health more.

As a wise philosopher once said, "The future is fluid, not frozen. It is constructed by our shifting and changing daily decisions, and each event influences all others... Change is not merely necessary to life—it is life."

If we maintain our self-awareness, we will ignore distractions. We keep to the principles of *Tao*.

The Book of Changes has never changed.

74. Traditional Chinese Medicine

Ancient medicine has come to the fore during the Covid-19 pandemic. Dr. Xia, from Wutongshan, and his volunteers, are a TCM rescue team organized with the financial aid of the Wanmingzi Philanthropic Foundation of Guangdong (funded by our company). This volunteer team has made great strides in the treatment and prevention of COVID-19 in Wuhan.

I have always believed that TCM is not only a medicine, but a philosophy. There are many things that cannot be explained on a purely physical level: perhaps modern medicine and the ancient principles of healing can achieve a closer integration.

Recently I experienced something amazing. With the help of a professor of traditional Chinese medicine—who used the traditional meridian acupuncture methods passed down by his ancestors—we managed to expel much of my body's toxins and excess weight. It took what seemed a very short time to remove the extra fat—close to a 70% reduction. This incredible effect was a surprise to me. I began to think deeply on the matter.

The history of traditional Chinese medicine goes back more than 5,000 years, to *Huangdi Neijing* (The Yellow Emperor's Classic of Medicine). In recent decades, we have lost so much of the treasure left to us by our ancestors. There's a reason for everything.

With the rapid development in urban life and creature comforts that come with material wealth, we in China have been experiencing a situation that mirrors the Western industrial revolution in the eighteenth century, which brought about drastic social changes. As large factories were constructed, pollution from smoke stacks made European cities and towns literally disappear; the work force began to move in large bodies to and from work at the same time each day; and people grew ill from breathing contaminated air. War accelerates the development of two major sciences: weapons and medicine. The large-scale trauma caused by the First World War (50 million dead) and the Second World War (80 million dead) created an urgent need for medicine that addressed mass injuries created by technologically advanced, highly destructive weapons. Both wars greatly therefore increased momentum in the development of Western medicine, whose treatment focuses on suppressing urgent physical symptoms.

Traditional Chinese medicine focuses on both the physical and spiritual aspects, and is based on the Yin/Yang theory: a dialectical treatment of both the symptoms and the root causes.

Some people ask: "Which is better, Western medicine or traditional Chinese medicine?" My answer is that both are good. They each have their own advantages and shortcomings. There is no absolute good or bad in all things, including human inventions and creations. As such, both systems should be symbiotic and complementary.

We must make good use of the advantages of Western medicine, which seeks to immediately address measurable injury; but we must also embrace the essence of traditional Chinese medicine, proven for over five thousand years. It can benefit human health on a level that addresses the invisible structures of energy not yet apparent to Western science. True, conventional medical treatment is unable to standardize the effects created by healing techniques—at least not in a way that it can measure according to its own definition of healing. But, each system can learn from the other's strong points to offset its own weaknesses. Western medicine can provide traditional Chinese medicine with testing procedures and standards, while traditional Chinese medicine can explain its holistic treatment protocols to the West. This binary approach will benefit the planet.

Western medicine is a hammer that sees everything as a nail. It kills viruses if there are viruses; it deploys antibiotics where it finds infections; it treats the head if the patient has a headache; it removes organs that are no longer functioning.

TCM takes the patient as a whole into account and aims to reach a balance of yin and yang. In nature, all must undergo the process of birth and growth and the dual effect of opposite forces at work simultaneously. If balance in the patient is achieved through the promotion and restraint of these opposites, and between the five elements, then disease can be treated successfully.

It is the worldview of the Chinese that people do not exist alone, and that all lives are associated with all other lives. We exist together in a close association with the universe. We are a circuitry on the Planet, and we connect to each other. The light that comes on in one, comes on in all.

The same concept applies to the individual physical body.

Huangdi Neijing believes that there is a system of channels in the human body: twelve main and collateral channels corresponding to the twelve periods of the day. If we can live our daily lives according to the rhythm of the twelve periods of the day, we will be endowed with energy. This is how *Tao* follows the way of nature in the simplest way. But the simpler things are, the more difficult it is to follow them. For example, sleeping early and eating little are good for the health, but modern people often do exactly the opposite.

Why is a simple thing so difficult to do? It is because "although the mind hopes to be calm, desires keep distracting it." TCM hopes to nourish good health, and the highest state of health is achieved by nourishing the mind. That's how ancient medicine cures people. It takes the body and mind and spirit into account.

Emotions can do great harm to a peaceful mind. Mental disturbances hinder the channels from running normally, which results in disease—literally, *dis-ease*. Therefore, when you do get sick, the first thing to do is to calm your mind. In that state, vital energy flows smoothly, the blood circulates freely, and good health is restored.

The disconnect between people and nature—and other people—is the root of our personal, social and ecological problems. In a broad sense, traditional Chinese medicine is also the cure for what ails a country.

That's why the ancient Chinese said: "Be a good doctor if you cannot be a good prime minister." The way of curing people and the way of governing the country are both connected. The same methodology is employed.

An old German professor once regained good health thanks to ancient Chinese medicine. He recounted his experiences over sixty years. He stated that it was not only a system belonging to the Chinese people but a treasure belonging to mankind. It represents a metaphysical formlessness that connects the universe; it is a tool with specific features that can cure; and finally, it is an outlook, the world view of a culture—the art and philosophy and values of daily life in the Orient—a lifestyle that conforms to *Tao*.

75. Knowing and Doing

Once a day, the black of the sky pales ever so slightly on the horizon. The stars are still shining brightly, and the constellations and the drama associated with them are stretched above us like old stories read on the pages of the night. The horizon turns yellow and the planet Venus is visible as it accompanies the sun, that giant star that is our friend, as it breaches the surface of the earth. The stars fade, but they have gone nowhere. And all the planets are where they should be. For the hours of daylight, the light of the sun will hide them.

At this time of day, everywhere we look is filled with freshness and energy; the world is enlivened. Birds of different types sing the same series of notes repeatedly. People wake, houselights come on, and the world becomes active.

The ancients said, "An hour in the morning is worth two in the evening." Our group starts the day by reading the *Tao Te Ching* for the same reason. Our state of mind in the morning determines our state of mind for the rest of the day. By reading the *Tao Te Ching*, we commence the day in a concentrated state of mind, with a positive energy.

It is what happens in nature. We mirror it.

At the beginning of a new day, we should, according to *Tao*, "do nothing against the way of nature but do the things nature needs us to do." What matters is that reading the book helps us remove distracting thoughts and the drain on energy that accompanies such thoughts. We focus on the reading.

Year in, year out, as we repeat this process, the sentences in the book are naturally engraved on the mind. Time passes quietly in reading, making those thirty minutes meaningful, valuable, and fruitful.

Cultivation as I use it means refinement and training: the unity of knowledge and action. The process of applying the classics to daily life and to work is a way of achieving that unity. If it is not performed daily, the cycle that is part of nature would be broken. It is as if the sun did not come up one day.

The key to practice is persistence without a break, because taking breaks means a disconnection of energy, which leads to a disruption of the process. Our previous efforts are wasted. That's why truly determined people will memorize the content and recite it whenever they can. No matter how noisy the external environment is, all we need to do is to focus on the classics. On a surface level, some Western life coaches advise their clients to do the same—by repeating key aphorisms that in turn reinforce positive thinking.

As time passes, our wisdom grows, and we comprehend the classics more. We achieve a unity of knowing and doing—through reading and recitation. We naturally apply the principles of *Tao* without giving it too much thought, because it becomes part of our thought process.

76. The Small Goal of Longevity

As a child, I tended to be restless and depressed. I felt lost. Everything seemed gray to me. As a result, I experienced many health issues, including palpitations, gastroenterological disturbances, and insomnia.

If I did not need a lesson in the connection of mind and body, I got it then.

The *Tao Te Ching* says, "There is no relationship that cannot be properly conducted." If a person can handle family relationships well, he should be able to negotiate relationships with others in his life as well as between superiors and subordinates. None of us has come into the world to live alone. No man is an island.

The remedial action we can take immediately is to change ourselves.

Now I have become older—and healthier.

One of my friends is a doctor. He told me that my organs were healthy and vital—healthier than many young people. Since founding the company, I have been under great pressure and my schedule is constantly tight, making a regular routine difficult.

Yet I have become healthier as time passes.

As stated previously, disease is closely connected with the mind. Even when people live in the same environment and eat the same food, some are healthy, and others get sick.

Different states of mind.

Advanced technology has created convenience. People are gradually losing self-discipline in eating, in resting, and in the pursuit of desire, and ill-health is becoming more prevalent.

Cause and effect applies to health as it does elsewhere: the harmony between mind and body. At a spiritual level, we should maintain a healthy and charitable mind that takes pleasure from good actions; while at the physical level, we should stop blindly believing that aerobic exercise will bring us health, and instead find the most effective method of nourishing the body, depending on our specific chemistry. Running ten kilometers a day may have certain benefits, but it will certainly wear down your joints. Ask any long-distance runner.

I have set a small goal of longevity, and I believe I can achieve it. My clothes have shrunk from XL to XS. (I practice the self-restrain I preach.) I have adopted certain practices in behavior and mindfulness. When I integrate these into my day, my worries vanish—because I do not obsess on them.

A tranquil mind is a cure for many of life's ailments.

I learned this as a child. It is true today.

77. Breaking Barriers

The morning sessions have won me a new title: Teacher Ma, or Ma Laoshi. These are in addition to "Chairman" and "Director." I do worry a little that I am not worthy of this title. However, it has encouraged me to keep a broad vision of what it means to be an active person.

People say they are inspired by what I share in writing.

I have been interested in books since a child, including biographies of great people, and Western philosophy. When I was running the medical cosmetology institute, I avoided solely relying on my familial inheritance of ancient medicine: I also widely read professional books on TCM and Western medicine. As a result, the institute did quite well.

On my many career paths, despite wide reading, I never found a way that made sense to me until reading the Chinese classics. I had previously believed that the Buddhist concept of "barriers of knowing" were barriers caused by knowing too much. That's not the case. Wide learning will not necessarily cause barriers; those emerge when we become overwhelmed with our acquired knowledge and our prejudices. For example, if I had become consumed with what I learned in Western philosophy, how could I adopt a wisdom totally contrary to the ideals and beliefs I had before?

Try not to be closed to new things—that attitude will hinder your development and understanding of the wider world.

Many inexperienced young people are especially obsessed with short-term facts and opinions. They don't know how to put themselves in another person's shoes. They are consequently conceited and prejudiced regarding the issues of the day. If they hear an opinion that differs from theirs, they instinctively reject it instead of exploring the merits of that opinion.

Here is a name for the big barrier: "My View."

Once we understand this, we realize that Buddhism does not say "do not learn," but rather not to be consumed with what we learn.

Keep an emptiness inside to embrace the new.

Nothing can be put into a glass if the glass is already filled.

To be a truly cultured person, we try our best to acquire wisdom, knowledge, self-awareness, and the capacity to see things in a different light.

Don't assert categorically. Pride and Prejudice are barriers to Knowing.

The universe is a mysterious process of change and substance, about which humans know little. Surely we must learn to respect the way of Nature, to listen with an open mind, to be prudent in our pronouncements, and careful in our conduct.

The *Tao Te Ching* has already taught us: "do not reveal ourselves, do not justify ourselves, do not boast, nor be proud." It advises us to "round off the sharp edges, untie the knots, even the light and cool the turmoil."

78. Jun Porcelain

The magical coloring, the glaze on these rare minerals that have been buried for millennia.

They are lively in their effect, mysterious in their process of manufacture, and very difficult to duplicate. According to an old saying, one piece of exquisite Jun porcelain is the equivalent of a fortune.

Among many kinds of porcelains, it is my favorite.

The production rate of Jun porcelain is extremely low because it involves 72 steps, and the slightest mistake in any of those steps can render the entire process void. Since ancient times, a "curse" exists that nine out of ten kilns are destined to be failures—hence a local saying that "the shape (of a Jun porcelain) depends on the modeling, but its life depends on the firing."

Porcelain with the same color when entering the furnace may acquire a thousand different shades after the firing. Given the complicated techniques in manufacture, and the fact that the kiln reaches a thousand degrees, the coloring that takes place cannot be controlled by the people who make it. The colors that result make each piece of Jun porcelain a unique work of art that can never be duplicated.

Both its unpredictable appearance of the final result and the number of veins produced is part of Jun porcelain categorization and nomenclature. As night falls, it can continue with its "glaze cracking"; a process that can last sixty years. The most accurate description? It looks as if it has "been cracked by a hammer; yet upon touching, is perfectly smooth."

These features have enabled it to transcend rigidity and manual "control." It reflects a Will and a Spirit akin to that of a creator. The essential characteristic of Jun porcelain is Nature itself—a formlessness in compliance with *Tao* and yet a natural formation of its own. Thus its value.

The Yishou Vase is a work by Mr. Jin Peizhang, a master of Jun porcelain. We have it displayed in our Yuanfeng Life-style Hall. The vase is jade-like in color, like a lively spring. It is elegant and serene. Upon close observation, it looks un-earthly—an integration of the light and color of the Cosmos. Master Peizhang has dedicated his life to the art of Jun pottery. He has spent everything he has to build kilns for experiments, and he has returned to light the technique that dates from the Song Dynasty. He is an artisan, an embodiment of art and vir-tue, refined over decades.

Beauty rarely exists that is easily found everywhere. Jun porcelain embodies the unity of Man and Nature. I display the vases in the hope that those destined to see it will be inspired.

To compliment Porcelain Jun is Redwood Furniture in my office.

Years ago, when I first walked into the exhibition hall of Redwood furniture, I saw office desks made of old mahogany, big leaf and lobular sandalwood. I was immediately attracted by their invisible force. I stopped and took the time to appre-ciate them. The longer I looked, the more beautiful they be-came; the more I touched them, the more unwilling I was to leave.

Three kinds of Redwood: old mahogany, big leaf sandal-wood, and lobular red sandalwood.

Quiet, stable and steady. I touched them. They felt smooth and soft, like skin. Without paint, and carved with fine grinding, they displayed their natural charm.

The mahogany and sandalwood trees take centuries—even millennia—to mature. After five hundred years, they must have absorbed such a tremendous force from the universe.

They will have known numberless days swaying in wind and rain.

Roasting under a scorching sun. Thousands of years of Heaven and Earth, transformed in the hands of skilled craftsmen into the various attitudes of furniture, this form of life that has been forged over thousands of years. It is like a soul that remains steadfast.

Introverted, dignified, elegant.

They penetrate the soul without a word. They murmur gently in themes of old literature: *The Red Chamber*, *Three Kingdoms*, and *Outlaws of the Marsh*. Though pieces of furniture, I sensed the tenderness behind their tenacity, the sweet words in their silences. At the moment when I hold their handrails, they convey rivers, lakes, seas and miles of waves to me. I hear them swaying in the wind, tall and straight in the rain, and sense the shadow they provided from the hot sun over the centuries of growth. The sounds of a Redwood forest are something to marvel at. It is a vibration that can awaken a soul.

They will be blown by wind, drenched by rain, seared by sun. Most people do not read the profound writing in their serenity, the poetic dignity, or feel the spiritual sense in all that elegance. Yet their appearance alone is enough for most people to love what they are, and for men of letters to be intimate with them, and for collectors to indulge in them.

To enjoy thousands of scenes in hundreds of stories, and to endow them with all kinds of sentiments, the redwood furniture tells me their tales in my office.

79. Remembered and Hidden

History is very selective about the people it remembers. Sometimes, people have to remind history that it has missed a name.

I write this paragraph to give context to the times:

The years after the Second World War were fraught with international tension. Scientists from Germany, some of whom were in the German military, were brought to America to work on an atomic bomb. The Soviet Union was close behind, working with other German scientists. Given the horrors China had experienced in the years preceding that war, and the rapidly mounting tensions near its borders, the country could not allow itself to stand defenseless. It had to develop an atomic bomb. But the science was difficult and extremely dangerous. The stakes were high—the survival of the country itself.

One day, a 34-year-old husband parted from his wife and his young child. He drove to a secret location and entered a desert without even looking back.

For twenty-eight years he worked day and night on research. He persevered, despite the danger. Finally, a mushroom cloud in the sky signaled that China had its own atomic bomb.

Families wouldn't exist without country. And behind the grand concept of a "big country" is the happiness and sorrow of countless "small families."

A 30-year-old wife's husband had been assigned to a national classified project, of which she had no knowledge. She didn't know where he was going, what he was going to do, and what dangers he would face—nor when he would return home, if ever.

What she did know was that she needed to take care of their son and wait for him. That was her lonely mission, and sometimes she must have felt as if she were traveling alone through space in a small capsule, lost to the world. But with commitment and love, she completed her mission.

Ten thousand sleepless nights. Tears that cannot be counted.

A friend of mine sent me a video of Mr. Deng Jiaxian and his wife, Ms. Xu Luxi. Watching the video, I was deeply moved. These were two people who stayed together while apart. And although they were lost to distance and circumstances, they always had a place in each other's hearts.

When the couple was finally able to reunite, Mr. Deng was 61 years old. He was no longer the man who left her all those years ago, the man she remembered on those sleepless nights. Radiation had sickened him. He suffered great pain. He had 363 days to live.

When they met again, Xu Luxi tightly held Deng's hands.

He held his wife's hands.

The two of them had loved each other all of their lives, and although they were apart for such a long time, their lives were always one life.

At the end of the video, Deng Jiaxian says: "The future was worth my dedication."

Xu Luxi respond: "You were worth my waiting."

This is the character of the older generation to which Deng Jiaxian and his wife belonged.

Mr. Deng made a great contribution to China's first "two bombs," and is a national hero now known to history. He represents the country.

Although she spent her life waiting for him, she has not been visible in that history. She represents the family. The silent sacrifice made by this patriotic couple, captured in this deeply authentic film, has graced us.

We remember them both.

80. Cultivation Begins with the Mind

I remember when I first started my business in Shenzhen: I was on my way to the office one day: the sun was shining brightly. However, when I stepped off the bus, it began to rain heavily. I was drenched. I wondered what to do. Go home for a change of clothes, or go to the office? When I thought of the plans for the day ahead and the clients who had set up appointments, I realized that I must meet the clients.

Integrity. Responsibility.

As soon as I got to the office, I dried my hair with a towel and borrowed an electric dryer from the neighbor to dry my clothes. After all this was done, I began my day in a relaxed frame of mind.

Forewarned is forearmed. Over the past years, I have had the habit of working according to set plans. However, as my career path widens, there are inevitable accidents and emergencies.

One can easily get upset when plans are interrupted. My first reaction is always to ask myself: Did I really achieve a unity of knowledge and action? This question immediately calms me. At night, when I reflect upon it, I ask myself how people remain calm and unhurried in the midst of pressing affairs and do their job in an orderly fashion.

This is indeed a test for a person's state of mind. The ability to compartmentalize. To break a task into small tasks, as described in the *Tao*.

Rumination is a negative energy that doesn't do anyone any good. Whatever happens, we must accept it.

Our mindset determines our attitude, which determines our behavior, which influences our personality, which eventually determines success in life.

Whoever you are, whatever you are doing and whatever you wish for, this is the first lesson: cultivate the mind.

Once you formulate a positive state of mind, your thoughts will be just and kind by nature. This positive energy produced eventually helps you to handle all sorts of situations with ease.

It is not a mysterious process.

According to Buddhism, all things are but creations of our mind.

Our world is created by the mind, and likewise, all the things we have are created by the mind.

If you are sunlight, your world is warm; if you are love, your life is filled with love; if you are happiness, you live in joy. When we complain about our lives, it's not our lives but we who have failed us.

That what's expressed in the phrase, "If you seek for things and don't get them, seek the cause in yourself." Therefore, the transformation of society must begin with a transformation in people's minds.

81. A Violet or a Rose?

In a quiet garden by a wall, a violet hides in green grass, content with her life. Such a contentment has sheltered her from storms. The violet has never dreamed about other gorgeous, unique flowers.

In the quiet of the night, she hears a voice: "Ambition beyond existence is the essential purpose of our being." The violet then desires to achieve a state higher than her own, and to become a rose for one day. The clan of other violets laugh. The rose tells her to be happy: "The exalted will be crushed."

However, she holds onto her dream, until Nature finally grants her wish. She is transformed from a small violet by a corner wall into a rose, rising above all other flowers in the garden.

For a day, she lives a glorious life.

But she has lost her ability to stay close to the ground.

When a violent storm lays waste to the garden, only the violets survive. The new rose has been hurled to the ground, her stem broken.

In the last moments of her life, she says to the other violets: "I could have lived the same life you are living now by clinging with fear to the earth. I am happy now because I have probed outside my little world into the mystery of the Universe…something which you have not yet done…I have looked at the Universe from behind the eyes of a rose."

Very frail, she says: "I shall die now, for my soul has attained its goal. But my soul has experienced something a violet has never experienced. I have finally extended my knowledge to a world beyond the narrow cavern of my birth. This is the design of Life."

This is the story of "The Ambitious Violet" written by Khalil Gibran, the Lebanese writer. The spirit of the violet to do her utmost for the realization of her dream has deeply touched readers.

In the first years of my path in business, I took a severe beating from the cruelty and coldness of life. There were moments when I was totally lost, not knowing whether I should give up or keep going. However, I clung to my dream and resolutely pursued it.

Some say: "There are two kinds of people: those who think it's enough to live a stable life like everybody else, and those who challenge fate and fight for a dream. They pursue beauty deep in their souls, and they eventually transform themselves."

I hope I have had the courage to challenge my fate and to pursue truth and beauty. Anyone who has dreams in the heart will inevitably experience sufferings and setbacks, because that's how the soul is forged and shaped.

Is it better to be a violet, hiding in the corner and waiting for the time to safely pass until winter inevitably comes, or to take a chance and become a proud and beautiful rose?

The question is mine: the answer is yours.

THE END

The Translators/Editors

Gerard Donovan was born in Ireland and is a graduate of the prestigious Writing Seminars at The Johns Hopkins University in Maryland, USA. His first novel was a Barnes & Noble *Discover Great New Writers* pick and was nominated for the Booker Prize. His third novel, *Julius Winsome*, became an international success, appearing in fourteen languages. Newspapers around the world hailed it as a masterpiece. *The New Yorker* said: "Donovan delivers with devastating force," and *The Financial Times* called it "Enormously resonant and beautiful." A Mandarin edition is forthcoming. Until 2017 he was a Reader in English at Plymouth University, England.

Dr Jeannie Jinsheng Yi is the author of several influential business books on corporate culture and corporate governance. *The Haier Way* was recommended by the US Chamber of Commerce to American CEOs traveling to China. Dr Yi has acted as an international consultant on entertainment and financial projects that bridge China and the West. She has brought Twentieth Century Fox and Village Roadshow to China to create IP-based theme parks. She currently serves as co-executive producer of the 24th Family Film Awards as it grows from its American roots and reaches a truly global audience.

She received her PhD in Literature from Washington University in St Louis.